THE HERMITAGE PSALTER

REVISED DOUAY VERSION

THE HERMITAGE

PSALTER

REVISED DOUAY VERSION

ErCam Editions
Bloomingdale, Ohio

Nihil Obstat and Imprimatur:
Very Reverend Elias Castillo, Er. Cam., Superior Major
Pentecost Sunday, 2023

In Memoria:
Father Basil, Er. Cam., Prior
Pentecost Sunday, 2023

Cover art: King David fresco, in the Basilica of San Vitale,
by Tarquinio Ligustri (1603)
Back cover color image, courtesy of the Hermitage of the Five Martyrs,
Bieniszew, Poland

ISBN 979-8-9855649-0-7
Library of Congress Control Number: 2022909622

Sold by: faithandfamily.pub

Printed in the United States of America

BOOK I

Psalms 1-41

(The tribulations of Davi•)

Psalm 1

Beatus vir

Two ways and two ends (cf. Matthew 7:24-27)

* 1 Blessed is the man
who hath not walked in the counsel of the wicked,
* nor stood in the way of sinners,
nor sat in the seat of scoffers;
* 2 but his will is in the law of the LORD,
and in His law will he meditate day and night.

* 3 And he shall be like a tree †
transplanted by streams of water,
which shall give its fruit in its season,
* and its leaf shall not fall off;
and all that he doeth shall prosper.

* 4 Not so are the wicked, not so, †
but they are like chaff,
which the wind driveth away.

* 5 Therefore the wicked shall not stand in the judgment,
nor sinners in the council of the just.
* 6 For the LORD knoweth the way of the just,
but the way of the wicked shall perish.

Psalm 2

Quare fremuerunt gentes

The Lord and His Christ shall rule all nations (Acts 4:25-26)

* 1 Why have the Gentiles raged,
and the peoples meditated vanity?
* 2 The kings of the earth have taken their stand, †
and the rulers have gathered together
against the LORD and against His Anointed:
* 3 "Let us break their bonds asunder
and cast their cords from us."

* 4 He Who dwelleth in the heavens shall laugh;
the LORD shall mock at them.
* 5 Then He shall speak to them in His anger,
and dismay them in His fury:
* 6 "I Myself have appointed My king
on Zion, My holy mountain."

* 7 I will declare the decree of the LORD. †
He said to me, "Thou art My Son,
this day have I begotten thee.
* 8 Ask of Me, and I will give thee †
the Gentiles for thy inheritance,
and the ends of the earth for thy possession.
* 9 Thou shalt rule them with a rod of iron,
dash them in pieces like a potter's vessel."

* 10 And now, O kings, be prudent;
be instructed, you that judge the earth.
* 11 Serve the LORD with fear,
and exult ye with trembling.
* 12 Kiss the Son, lest he be angry, †
and you perish in the way,
for his anger is quickly kindled.

* Blessed are all
that take refuge in Him.

Psalm 3

Domine, qui• multiplicati

A man with God against a multitude (cf. 2 Samuel 15:12b)

1 *A Psalm of Davi•, when he fle• from Absalom his son.*

* 2 O LORD, how my adversaries have multiplied!
Many are rising up against me;
* 3 many are saying of my soul,
"There is no salvation for him in God." *Selah*

* 4 But Thou, O LORD, art a shield about me,
my glory and the lifter up of my head.
* 5 With my voice I called upon the LORD,
and He answered me from His holy mountain. *Selah*

* 6 I laid me down and slept;
I awoke, for the LORD upholdeth me.
* 7 I will not fear myriads of people,
that beset me on every side.

* Arise, O LORD; save me, O my God, †
8 for Thou hast struck all my enemies on the cheek;
Thou hast broken the teeth of the wicked.

* 9 Salvation belongeth to the LORD;
Thy blessing be upon Thy people. *Selah*

Psalm 4

Cum invocarem

Peace at night

1 *To the choirmaster: with strings. A Psalm of David.*

* 2 When I call, hearken to me, O God of my justice. †
Thou madest room for me when I was in straits;
be gracious to me and hear my prayer.

* 3 O sons of man, how long shall my glory be dishonoured?
How long will you love vanity and seek after
falsehood? *Selah*
* 4 But know that the LORD hath set apart the godly man
for Himself;
the LORD will hear me when I call to Him.

* 5 Be angry and sin not;
speak in your hearts upon your beds and be still. *Selah*
* 6 Offer the sacrifices of justice,
and trust in the LORD.

* 7 Many say, "Who will shew us good?"
Lift up on us the light of Thy countenance, O LORD.
* 8 Thou hast put more gladness into my heart
than when their grain and wine abound.

* 9 In peace I will both lay me down and sleep,
for Thou alone, O LORD, makest me dwell in safety.

Psalm 5

Verba mea auribus

Morning offering

1 *To the choirmaster. For the flutes. A Psalm of David.*

* 2 Give ear to my words, O LORD;
consider my meditation.
* 3 Attend to the voice of my cry for help,
my king and my God.

* 4 For to Thee will I pray, O LORD.
In the morning Thou shalt hear my voice.
* In the morning I will set in order a sacrifice to Thee,
and I will watch.

* 5 For Thou art not a God Who willest wickedness;
evil shall not sojourn with Thee;
* 6 the boastful shall not stand
before Thy eyes.
* 7 Thou hatest all wrongdoers; †
Thou destroyest those that speak lies;
the LORD abhorreth the man of blood and deceit.

* 8 But I, in the abundance of Thy mercy,
will enter into Thy house.
* I will adore toward Thy holy temple
in Thy fear.

* 9 Lead me, O LORD, in Thy justice †
because of my adversaries;
make straight Thy way before my face.

* 10 For there is nothing reliable in their mouth;
their heart is a pit;
* their throat is an open sepulchre;
they make smooth their tongues.

* 11 Declare them guilty, O God;
let them fall by their own counsels.
* Because of the multitude of their transgressions
thrust them out,
for they have rebelled against Thee.

* 12 But let all that take refuge in Thee rejoice;
let them shout for joy forever;
* Thou shalt protect them, and they shall exult in Thee,
those that love Thy name.

* 13 For Thou wilt bless the just, O LORD;
Thou wilt surround him with good will as with a shield.

Psalm 6

Domine, ne in furore

Illness, a divine rebuke and discipline (v. 2 = 38: 2)
(First Penitential Psalm)

1 *To the choirmaster: with strings; on the eighth. A Psalm of David.*

* 2 O LORD, rebuke me not in Thy anger,
nor discipline me in Thy wrath.

* 3 Be gracious to me, O LORD, for I am weak; †
heal me, O LORD,
for my bones are dismayed.
* 4 And my soul is sorely dismayed;
but Thou, O LORD, how long?

* 5 Turn, O LORD, deliver my soul;
save me for Thy mercy's sake.
* 6 For in death there is no remembrance of Thee;
in hell, who shall confess to Thee?

* 7 I am weary with my groaning. †
Every night I flood my bed;
I drench my couch with my tears.

* 8 My eye is wasted because of grief;
it groweth old because of all my adversaries.

* 9 Depart from me, all ye wrongdoers,
for the LORD hath heard the voice of my weeping.
* 10 The LORD hath heard my supplication;
the LORD will receive my prayer.

* 11 All my enemies shall be ashamed and very troubled;
they shall turn back, suddenly ashamed.

Psalm 7

Domine, Deus meus

"God the judge of all" (Hebrews 12:23)

1 *A lamentation of Davi•, which he sang to the LORD because of Cush the Benjaminite.*

* 2 O LORD my God, in Thee have I taken refuge;
save me from all my pursuers and deliver me,
* 3 lest one of them tear my soul like a lion,
rending, with none to deliver.

* 4 O LORD my God, if I have done this,
if there is injustice in my hands,
* 5 if I requited him with evil who was at peace with me,
I who released my adversary for nothing,
* 6 let the enemy pursue my soul and overtake it, †
and trample my life to the ground,
and lay my glory in the dust. *Selah*

* 7 Arise, O LORD, in Thy anger;
exalt Thyself against the fury of my adversaries,
* and awake, O my God:
Thou hast commanded a judgment.

* [8] And the congregation of the peoples shall gather round Thee, †
and Thou sit enthroned above it on high:
[9] The LORD judgeth the peoples.

* Judge me, O LORD, according to my justice
and according to my integrity, that is in me.
* [10] O let the evil of the wicked come to an end,
but establish Thou the just;
* for the trier of hearts and reins
is the just God.

* [11] My shield is upon God,
Who saveth the upright of heart.
* [12] God is a just judge,
and a God Who is indignant every day.

* If a man will not repent, †
[13] He will whet His sword;
He hath bent His bow and made it ready.
* [14] And He hath prepared for Himself deadly weapons,
making His arrows fiery shafts.

* [15] Behold one who was in travail with wrong,
and conceived trouble, and brought forth falsehood.
* [16] He dug a pit and hollowed it out,
and he is fallen in the pit which he made.
* [17] His trouble shall return upon his head,
and on his own pate shall his violence descend.

* [18] I will thank the LORD according to His justice
and sing a psalm to the name of the LORD the Most High.

Psalm 8

Domine, Dominus noster

The anthropic principle: All is for man

1 *To the choirmaster. Accor• ing to the "Gittith." A Psalm of Davi•.*

* 2 O LORD, our Lord,
how magnificent is Thy name in all the earth!

* Thou hast set Thy majesty above the heavens. †
3 Out of the mouth of babes and sucklings,
Thou hast perfected praise,
* because of Thy adversaries,
to still the enemy and the avenger.

* 4 When I see the heavens, the work of Thy fingers,
the moon and the stars, which Thou hast established,
* 5 what is man, that Thou art mindful of him,
or the son of man, that Thou visitest him?

* 6 Thou hast made him a little lower than the angels;
with glory and honour Thou hast crowned him.
* 7 Thou hast given him dominion over the works of Thy hands;
Thou hast put all things under his feet:
* 8 All sheep and oxen,
and also the beasts of the field,
* 9 the birds of heaven and the fish of the sea,
whatever passeth along the paths of the sea.

* 10 O LORD, our Lord,
how magnificent is Thy name in all the earth!

Psalm 9

Confitebor tibi, Domine

The Lord will vindicate the oppressed

1 *To the choirmaster. To the mode of the song "Muth-labben."*
A Psalm of David.

* 2 I will confess to Thee, O LORD, with all my heart;
I will recount all Thy wonders.
* 3 I will be glad and exult in Thee;
I will sing a psalm to Thy name, O Most High.

* 4 When my enemies turn back,
they stumble and perish before Thy face.
* 5 For Thou hast maintained my judgment and my cause;
Thou hast sat on the throne, judging justly.

* 6 Thou hast rebuked the heathen, destroyed the wicked;
Thou hast blotted out their name forever and ever.
* 7 The enemy have ended in everlasting ruins, †
and their cities Thou hast uprooted;
their very memory hath perished.

* 8 But the LORD shall sit enthroned forever;
He hath established his throne for judgment.
* 9 And He will judge the world with justice;
He will judge the peoples with equity.

* 10 And the LORD shall be a high place for the oppressed,
a high place in times of distress.
* 11 And those that know Thy name will trust Thee,
for Thou hast not forsaken them that seek Thee, O LORD.

* 12 Sing psalms to the LORD, Who dwelleth in Zion;
declare His deeds among the peoples.

* 13 For requiring their blood, He hath remembered them;
He hath not forgotten the cry of the poor!

* 14 Be gracious to me, O LORD; †
see my affliction from those that hate me,
Thou that liftest me up from the gates of death,
* 15 that I may tell all Thy praise †
at the gates of the daughter of Zion,
that I may exult in Thy salvation.

* 16 The heathen have sunk into the pit which they made;
in the net which they hid is their own foot taken.
* 17 The LORD hath manifested Himself, executing judgment;
the wicked is snared in the work of his own hands.
Higgaion. Selah

* 18 The wicked shall be turned back towards hell,
all the nations that forget God.
* 19 For the needy shall not always be forgotten;
the expectation of the poor shall not perish forever.

* 20 Arise, O LORD, let not man prevail;
let the heathen be judged in Thy sight.
* 21 Put them in fear, O LORD;
let the heathen know they are but men. *Selah*

Psalm 10 (9:22-39)

Ut quid, Domine

"And it was given to the beast to make war with the saints"
(Apocalypse 13:7)

* 1 Why, O LORD, dost Thou stand afar off?
Why hidest Thou Thyself in times of trouble?
* 2 In pride, the wicked hotly pursue the poor;
let them be caught in the schemes they have devised.

* 3 For the wicked boasteth of the desires of his soul,
and he calleth the covetous blessed.
* 4 The wicked spurneth the LORD in the pride of his
countenance: †
"He will not require it; there is no God,"
5 such are all his thoughts.

* His ways prosper at all times. †
Thy judgments are on high, out of his sight;
as for all his adversaries, he puffeth at them.
* 6 He hath said in his heart, "I shall not be moved;
from generation to generation I shall never suffer evil."

* 7 His mouth is full of cursing, and deceit, and oppression;
under his tongue are trouble and wrong.
* 8 He sitteth in ambush in the villages;
in secret places he killeth the innocent.
* 9 His eyes watch for the hapless;
he lurketh in secret like a lion in his lair.
* He lurketh, that he may seize the poor;
he seizeth the poor, when he draweth him into his net.

* 10 The poor is crushed, he sinketh down,
and so the hapless fall by his strength.
* 11 He hath said in his heart, "God hath forgotten;
He hath turned away His face, He will never see."

* 12 Arise, O LORD; †
O God, lift up Thy hand;
forget not the poor!

* 13 Why doth the wicked spurn God?
For he hath said in his heart, "He will not require it."

* 14 Thou hast seen: †
for Thou considerest trouble and vexation,
to take them into Thy hands.
* The hapless abandoneth himself to Thee;
Thou hast been the helper of the fatherless.

* 15 Break the arm of the wicked and the evil;
search out his wickedness till none be found.
* 16 The LORD is king forever and ever:
the heathen shall perish from His land.

* 17 The desire of the poor Thou hast heard, O LORD;
Thou wilt establish their heart, Thou wilt incline Thy ear,
* 18 to execute judgment for the fatherless and the oppressed,
so that man, who is of the earth, may terrify no more.

Psalm 11 (10)

In Domino confi•o

Human life a trial (cf. Job 7:17-18)

1 *To the choirmaster. Of Davi•.*

* In the LORD have I taken refuge; †
how do you say to my soul:
“Flee like a bird to the mountain.

* 2 For lo, the wicked bend the bow; †
they have made ready their arrow upon the string,
to shoot in the dark at the upright of heart.
* 3 When the foundations are being torn down,
what can the just man do?”

* 4 The LORD is in His holy temple;
the LORD’s throne is in heaven.
* His eyes behold, His eyelids try,
the children of men.

* 5 The LORD trieth the just and the wicked,
and the lover of violence His soul hateth.
* 6 He shall rain coals of fire and brimstone on the wicked,
and a raging wind shall be the portion of their cup.

* 7 For the LORD is just, and He loveth just deeds;
the upright shall behold His face.

Psalm 12 (11)

Salvum me fac

Pure words in a world of lies

1 *To the choirmaster: on the eighth. A Psalm of David.*

* 2 Save, O LORD, for there is no longer any saint,
for the faithful fail from among the children of men.
* 3 They have spoken vain things, each one to his neighbour;
with smooth lips, with a double heart have they spoken.

* 4 The LORD shall cut off all smooth lips,
the tongue that speaketh great things.
* 5 Those who have said, "With our tongue we will prevail;
our lips are with us; who is lord over us?"

* 6 "Because the poor are despoiled, because the needy groan, †
now will I arise," saith the LORD:
"I will place him in the salvation for which he longeth."
* 7 The words of the LORD are pure words, †
silver refined in a furnace in the ground,
purified seven times.

* 8 Thou, O LORD, wilt keep us;
Thou wilt preserve us forever from this generation.
* 9 The wicked walk round about,
while vileness is exalted among the sons of men.

Psalm 13 (12)

Usquequo, Domine

"We hoped he would redeem Israel, but this is the third day"
(Luke 24: 21)

[1] *To the choirmaster. A Psalm of Davi•.*

* [2] How long, O LORD? Wilt Thou forget me forever?
How long wilt Thou turn away Thy face from me?
* [3] How long shall I take counsel in my soul, †
have sorrow in my heart by day?
How long shall my enemy be exalted over me?

* [4] Look and answer me, O LORD my God.
Enlighten my eyes, lest I sleep in death,
* [5] lest my enemy say, "I have prevailed against him,"
lest my adversaries exult that I am moved.

* [6] But I have trusted in Thy mercy.
My heart shall exult in Thy salvation.
* I will sing to the LORD,
because He hath dealt bountifully with me.

Psalm 14 (13)

Dixit insipiens

The folly of disbelief; the assured counsel of the poor

1 *To the choirmaster. Of David.*

* The fool hath said in his heart,
"There is no God."
* They are corrupt, they do abominable deeds;
there is none that doeth good.

* 2 The LORD looked down from heaven
upon the children of men
* to see if there was any that had insight,
that sought after God.

* 3 All have turned aside;
they are all alike corrupt.
* There is none that doeth good,
not even one.

* 4 Shall not all the wrongdoers know, †
who eat up My people as they eat bread?
They do not call upon the LORD.

* 5 There they were in great dread,
for God is with the just generation.
* 6 You would confound the counsel of the poor,
but the LORD is his refuge.

* 7 Who shall give the salvation of Israel out of Zion? †
When the LORD restoreth the fortunes of His people,
Jacob shall exult and Israel be glad.

Psalm 15 (14)

Domine, quis habitabit

The just shall dwell with God

1 *A Psalm of Davi•.*

* O LORD, who shall sojourn in Thy tabernacle?
Who shall dwell on Thy holy hill?

* 2 He that walketh in integrity, and doeth justice,
and speaketh the truth in his heart;
* 3 who hath not slandered with his tongue, †
nor done evil to his neighbour,
nor taken up a reproach against his near of kin.
* 4 In his eyes a reprobate is despised,
but he honoureth those that fear the LORD.

* Who hath sworn to his own hurt and changeth not, †
5 who hath not put out his money at interest,
nor taken a bribe against the innocent.

* He that doeth these things
shall never be moved.

Psalm 16 (15)

Conserva me, Domine

***Summum Bonum*: the Supreme Good**

1 *A miktam of Davi•.*

* Keep me, O God, for I have taken refuge in Thee. †
2 I have said to the LORD, "Thou art my Lord;
I have no good above Thee."

* 3 As for the saints that are in the land, †
they are the magnificent;
all my desire is for them.

* 4 Their sorrows shall be multiplied
that hasten after another god.
* I will not pour out their libations of blood,
nor will I take their names upon my lips.

* 5 The LORD is my allotted portion and my cup;
Thou holdest my lot.
* 6 The lines have fallen for me in pleasant places;
yea, I have a goodly heritage.

* 7 I will bless the LORD Who hath given me counsel;
even in the night my reins instruct me.
* 8 I have set the LORD always before me;
because He is at my right hand, I shall not be moved.

* 9 Therefore my heart is glad, and my glory exulteth;
my flesh, too, dwelleth in confidence.
* 10 For Thou wilt not abandon my soul to hell,
nor give Thy Merciful One to see corruption.

* 11 Thou wilt make known to me the paths of life, †
satisfaction of joys before Thy face,
pleasures at Thy right hand forever.

Psalm 17 (16)

Exaudi, Domine, justitiam

From spiritual combat to beatific vision

1 *A prayer of David.*

* Hear, O LORD, what is just;
attend to my outcry.
* Give ear to my prayer
from lips without deceit.
* 2 Let my judgment go forth from Thy presence;
let Thy eyes behold equity.

* 3 Thou hast tried my heart;
Thou hast visited me by night.
* Thou hast refined me by fire: †
Thou shalt find no scheming in me.
4 My mouth doth not transgress.
* As for the deeds of men, †
because of the words of Thy lips,
I have kept myself from the ways of the violent.
* 5 My steps have held fast to Thy paths;
my feet have not been moved.

* 6 I call upon Thee, †
for Thou wilt answer me, O God;
incline Thy ear to me, and hear my words.
* 7 Shew wondrously Thy mercies, O saviour of those
that take refuge from their assailants at Thy right hand.

* 8 Keep me as the apple of Thy eye;
hide me in the shadow of Thy wings,
* 9 from the face of the wicked, that overpower me.
My mortal enemies encompass me.

* 10 They are shut up in their fat;
with their mouth, they speak proudly.

* 11 Advancing, they now have surrounded me;
they set their eyes to cast me to the ground —
* 12 He is like a lion longing to tear,
and like a young lion crouching in secret places.

* 13 Arise, O LORD, confront him, bow him down;
deliver my soul from the wicked by Thy sword,
* 14 from men by Thy hand, O LORD,
from men whose portion in life is of the world.

* Thou fillest their belly with Thy treasure; †
their children are satisfied,
and they leave their surplus to their little ones.
* 15 But I in justice shall behold Thy face;
when I awake, I shall be satisfied with Thy form.

Psalm 18 (17)

Diligam te, Domine

The Lord's victory through David (cf. 2 Samuel 22)

1 *To the choirmaster. Of Davi•, the servant of the* LORD,
who spoke to the LORD *the wor•s of this canticle, when the* LORD
•elivere• him from the han• of all his enemies an• from the
han• of Saul.

2 *An• he sai•:*

* I love Thee, O LORD, my strength.
3 The LORD my rock, and my fortress, and my deliverer.
* My God, my rock — I will take refuge in Him —
my shield and the horn of my salvation; my high place.
* 4 I will call upon the LORD, Who is worthy to be praised,
and I will be saved from my enemies.

* 5 The cords of death surrounded me;
the torrents of Belial terrified me;
* 6 the cords of hell encompassed me;
the traps of death confronted me.

* [7] In my distress I called upon the LORD,
and to my God I cried for help.
* He heard my voice from His temple,
and my cry before Him entered His ears.

* [8] Then the earth heaved and quaked; †
the foundations of the mountains trembled
and heaved, because He was angry.
* [9] Smoke went up from His nostrils, †
and devouring fire from His mouth;
glowing coals flamed forth from Him.

* [10] He bowed the heavens and came down,
and gloom was under His feet.
* [11] And He rode on a cherub and did fly;
He soared upon the wings of the wind.

* [12] And He made darkness His secret place, †
His tabernacle round about Him,
dark waters, thick clouds of the sky.
* [13] From the brightness before Him †
thick clouds went ahead,
hailstones and coals of fire.

* [14] And the LORD thundered from the heavens, †
and the Most High gave forth His voice,
hailstones and coals of fire.
* [15] And He sent out His arrows and scattered them;
He shot out lightnings and routed them.

* [16] Then the channels of the sea were seen,
and the foundations of the world were laid bare
* at Thy rebuke, O LORD,
at the blast of the breath of Thy nostrils.
* [17] He sent forth from on high and took me;
He drew me out of many waters.

* [18] He delivered me from my strong enemies †
and from those that hated me,
for they were too steadfast for me.

* [19] They beset me in the day of my disaster,
but the LORD became my stay.
* [20] And He brought me forth into a broad place;
He delivered me, because He was well pleased with me.

* [21] The LORD rewarded me according to my justice;
according to the cleanness of my hands, He repaid me.
* [22] For I have kept the ways of the LORD,
and have not wickedly departed from my God.
* [23] For all His judgments are before me,
and His statutes I have not put away from me;
* [24] and I was blameless with Him,
and I kept myself from iniquity.
* [25] And the LORD repaid me according to my justice,
according to the cleanness of my hands before His eyes.

* [26] With the merciful Thou wilt show Thyself merciful,
with the blameless man Thou wilt show Thyself blameless,
* [27] with the pure Thou wilt show Thyself pure,
and with the twisted Thou wilt show Thyself complex.
* [28] For Thou wilt save a humble people,
but haughty eyes Thou wilt bring down.

* [29] For Thou lightest my lamp, O LORD;
my God doth lighten my darkness.
* [30] For by Thee I will run against a troop,
and by my God I will leap over a wall.

* [31] This God — His way is blameless;
the word of the LORD is refined.
* He is a shield
for all that take refuge in Him.

* [32] For who is God except the LORD?
Or who is a rock but our God?
* [33] The God Who girded me with strength,
and made my way blameless;
* [34] Who made my feet like hinds' feet
and made me stand upon the heights;

* 35 Who hath trained my hands for war,
and my arms to bend a bow of bronze.

* 36 And Thou gavest me the shield of Thy salvation, †
and Thy right hand upheld me,
and Thy humility made me great.
* 37 Thou didst widen my steps under me,
and my ankles did not totter.
* 38 I pursued my enemies and overtook them,
and did not turn back, till they were finished.
* 39 I smote them, so they could not rise;
they fell beneath my feet.

* 40 And Thou didst gird me with strength for the battle
and subdue under me those that rose up against me.
* 41 And my enemies, Thou didst make them turn their
backs to me,
and those that hated me I destroyed.
* 42 They cried for help, but there was none to save them,
to the LORD, but He answered them not.
* 43 So I beat them fine as dust before the wind;
I crushed them like the clay of the streets.

* 44 Thou didst deliver me from the strife of the people;
Thou didst make me the head of the Gentiles.
* A people I knew not served me;
45 at the hearing of the ear, they obeyed me.
* Foreigners feigned homage to me. †
46 Foreigners faded away
and came trembling out of their fastnesses.

* 47 The LORD liveth, and blessed be my rock,
and exalted be the God of my salvation.
* 48 The God Who giveth me vengeance †
and subdueth peoples under me,
Who delivereth me from my enemies.
* 49 Thou wilt indeed exalt me above those that rise up
against me;
from the violent man, Thou wilt deliver me.

* 50 Therefore will I confess to Thee, O LORD,
among the Gentiles,
and I will sing a psalm to Thy name,
* 51 Who doeth great deeds of salvation for His king, †
and performeth mercy for His anointed,
for David and his seed forever.

Psalm 19 (18)

Caeli enarrant

The glory of the heavens and the sweetness of the law

1 *To the choirmaster. A Psalm of Davi•.*

* 2 The heavens declare the glory of God,
and the firmament sheweth forth His handiwork.
* 3 Day unto day poureth forth speech,
and night unto night announceth knowledge.

* 4 There is no speech, nor are there words;
their voice is not heard:
* 5 Their voice hath gone out through all the earth,
and their words to the ends of the world.

* 6 In them He hath set a tabernacle for the sun, †
and he, as a bridegroom coming out of his chamber,
rejoiceth as a strong man to run his course.
* 7 His going forth is from the end of the heavens, †
and his circuit is to the end of them,
and nothing is hidden from his heat.

* 8 The law of the LORD is perfect,
converting the soul;
* the testimony of the LORD is faithful,
making wise the simple.
* 9 The precepts of the LORD are right,
rejoicing the heart;

* the commandment of the LORD is clear,
enlightening the eyes.
* 10 The fear of the LORD is pure,
abiding forever;
* the judgments of the LORD are truth,
just altogether.

* 11 They are more to be desired than gold,
even much fine gold;
* and sweeter are they than honey,
honey dripping from the comb.

* 12 Moreover, by them Thy servant is warned;
in keeping them, there is great reward.
* 13 Who can discern errors?
From hidden faults, clear me.

* 14 From presumptuous sins also keep Thy servant back;
let them not have dominion over me.
* Then shall I be blameless
and clear of great transgression.

* 15 May the words of my mouth
and the meditation of my heart
* be well-pleasing in Thy sight, O LORD,
my rock and my redeemer.

Psalm 20 (19)

Exau•iat te Dominus

God save the king

1 *To the choirmaster. A Psalm of Davi•.*

* 2 May the LORD answer thee in the day of trouble;
may the name of the God of Jacob set thee on high.

* 3 May He send thee help from the sanctuary,
and support thee from Zion.
* 4 May He remember all thy offerings,
and regard as fat all thy burnt sacrifices. *Selah*

* 5 May He give to thee according to thy heart,
and fulfill all thy counsel.
* 6 May we shout aloud at thy salvation, †
and in the name of our God raise up our banners;
may the LORD fulfill all thy petitions.

* 7 Now have I known
that the LORD hath saved His anointed.
* He will answer him from His holy heaven
with the mighty saving deeds of His right hand.

* 8 Some boast in chariots, and some in horses,
but we commemorate the name of the LORD our God.
* 9 They have bowed down and fallen,
but we have risen and stand upright.

* 10 O LORD, save the king,
and answer us on the day that we call.

Psalm 21 (20)

Domine, in virtute tua

The king's prayers answered

1 *To the choirmaster. A Psalm of Davi•.*

* 2 O LORD, in Thy strength the king is glad,
and in Thy salvation, how greatly doth he exult!
* 3 Thou hast given him his heart's desire;
Thou hast not withheld the wish of his lips. *Selah*

* 4 For Thou hast met him with goodly blessings;
Thou hast put on his head a crown of fine gold.
* 5 He asked life of Thee, and Thou gavest to him
length of days forever and ever.

* 6 Great is his glory through Thy salvation;
Thou layest upon him majesty and splendour.
* 7 For Thou makest him a blessing forever;
Thou dost gladden him with joy with Thy countenance.

* 8 For the king trusteth in the LORD,
and through the mercy of the Most High he shall
not be moved.
* 9 Thy hand shall find out all thy enemies,
thy right hand find out those that hate thee.

* 10 Thou shalt make them as a blazing oven
at the time of thy coming.
* The LORD shall swallow them up in His wrath,
and fire shall devour them.

* 11 Thou shalt destroy their fruit from the earth
and their seed from the children of men.
* 12 Though they intended evil against thee,
they devised schemes they cannot carry out.

* 13 For thou shalt make them turn back;
thou shalt aim thy bowstrings at their faces.
* 14 Be exalted, O LORD, in Thy strength;
we will sing and chant a psalm to Thy power.

Psalm 22 (21)

Deus, Deus meus

Passion and Resurrection foreseen (Matthew 27:46)

1 *To the choirmaster. Accor•ing to "The Hin• of the Dawn." A Psalm of Davi•.*

* 2 My God, my God, why hast Thou forsaken me?
Why art Thou far from my salvation and the words of my roaring?
* 3 O my God, I call by day, but Thou dost not answer,
and by night, but there is no stillness for me.

* 4 And yet, Thou art holy,
enthroned upon the praises of Israel.
* 5 In Thee our fathers trusted;
they trusted, and Thou didst deliver them.
* 6 To Thee they cried, and they escaped;
in Thee they trusted and were not confounded.

* 7 But I am a worm, and no man,
the reproach of men and despised by the people.
* 8 All that see me mock at me;
they curl their lips, they wag their heads.
* 9 "He committed himself to the LORD, let Him rescue him;
let Him deliver him, if He wanteth him."

* 10 For Thou art He Who drew me from the belly;
Thou didst make me secure upon my mother's breasts.
* 11 Upon Thee I was cast from the womb;
from my mother's belly Thou art my God.
* 12 Be not far from me, †
for trouble is near,
for there is none to help.

* 13 Many bullocks have encompassed me;
strong bulls of Bashan have surrounded me.

* [14] They have opened their mouths against me,
like a lion ravening and roaring.

* [15] I am poured out like water,
and all my bones are out of joint.
* My heart hath become like wax,
melted in the midst of my gut.
* [16] My strength is dried up like a potsherd, †
and my tongue cleaveth to my jaws,
and Thou layest me in the dust of death.

* [17] For dogs have surrounded me;
a band of evildoers have encompassed me.
* They have pierced my hands and my feet;
[18] I can count all my bones.
* They look, they stare at me; †
[19] they divide my garments among them,
and for my vesture, they cast lots.

* [20] But Thou, O LORD, be not far off;
O my strength, make haste to help me.
* [21] Deliver my soul from the sword,
my lonely self from the hand of the dog.
* [22] Save me from the mouth of the lion,
and from the horns of the wild oxen, answer me.

* [23] I will tell of Thy name to my brethren;
in the midst of the church, I will praise Thee.
* [24] Ye that fear the LORD, praise Him; †
all ye, the seed of Jacob, glorify Him,
and let all the seed of Israel stand in awe of Him.
* [25] For He hath not despised or abhorred
the poverty of the poor man,
* nor did He turn away His face from him,
but He heard, when he cried to Him.

* [26] From Thee is my praise in the great church;
I will pay my vows before those that fear Him.

* [27] The poor shall eat and be satisfied; †
they shall praise the LORD, those that seek Him.
May your hearts live forever.

* [28] All the ends of the earth
shall remember and return to the LORD,
* and all the families of the Gentiles
shall worship before Him.
* [29] For the kingdom is the LORD's,
and He shall rule over the Gentiles.

* [30] All the stalwart of the earth
will eat and will worship.
* Before His face will bow all †
who descend to the dust,
even he who cannot keep his soul alive.

* [31] Posterity shall serve Him. †
It shall be told of the Lord
to a generation yet to come,
* [32] and they shall declare His justice †
to a people yet to be born,
that He hath done it.

Psalm 23 (22)

Dominus regit me

"I am the good shepherd" (John 10: 11a)

1 *A Psalm of David.*

* The LORD is my shepherd;
I shall not want.

* 2 He maketh me to lie down in green pastures. †
He guideth me beside restful waters.
3 He restoreth my soul.
* He leadeth me in paths of righteousness
for His name's sake.

* 4 Even though I should walk †
through the valley of the shadow of death,
I will fear no evil,
* for Thou art with me;
Thy rod and Thy staff, they comfort me.

* 5 Thou spreadest a table before me
in the presence of my adversaries;
* Thou hast anointed my head with oil;
my cup runneth over.

* 6 Surely goodness and mercy shall pursue me
all the days of my life,
* and I shall dwell in the house of the LORD
for length of days.

Psalm 24 (23)

Domini est terra

The king of glory comes to the innocent

1 *A Psalm of David.*

* The earth is the LORD's, and the fulness thereof,
the world, and they that dwell therein,
* 2 for He hath founded it upon the seas,
and established it upon the rivers.

* 3 Who shall ascend the mountain of the LORD,
and who shall stand in His holy place?
* 4 The innocent of hands and the pure of heart, †
who hath not lifted up his soul unto vanity,
and hath not sworn deceitfully.

* 5 He shall receive a blessing from the LORD,
and justice from the God of his salvation.
* 6 Such is the generation of them that seek Him,
that seek the face of the God of Jacob. *Selah*

* 7 Lift up your heads, O ye gates, †
and be ye lifted up, O everlasting doors,
and the king of glory shall come in.

* 8 Who is this king of glory? †
The LORD, strong and mighty,
the LORD, mighty in battle.

* 9 Lift up your heads, O ye gates, †
and be ye lifted up, O everlasting doors,
and the king of glory shall come in.

* 10 Who is this king of glory? †
The LORD of hosts,
He is the king of glory. *Selah*

Psalm 25 (24)

Ad te, Domine, levavi

"Prayer is the ascent of the mind to God"

(St. John Damascene)

1 *A Psalm of David.*

* To Thee, O LORD, do I lift up my soul.
2 O my God, in Thee have I trusted;
* let me not be ashamed.
Let not my enemies exult over me.
* 3 Indeed, none that wait for Thee shall be ashamed.
They shall be ashamed that are wantonly false.

* 4 Make me know Thy ways, O LORD;
teach me Thy paths.
* 5 Make me walk in Thy truth and teach me, †
for Thou art the God of my salvation;
for Thee have I waited all the day.

* 6 Remember Thy compassionate deeds, O LORD,
and Thy mercies, for they are from of old.
* 7 Remember not the sins of my youth and my transgressions; †
according to Thy mercy, remember Thou me,
for Thy goodness' sake, O LORD.

* 8 Good and upright is the LORD;
therefore will He instruct sinners in the way.
* 9 He will make the meek walk in judgment,
and He will teach the meek His way.

* 10 All the paths of the LORD are mercy and truth,
to those that observe His covenant and His testimonies.
* 11 For Thy name's sake, O LORD,
pardon my iniquity, though it is great.

* [12] Who is the man that feareth the LORD?
He will instruct him in the way that he should choose.
* [13] His soul shall abide in good,
and his seed shall inherit the land.
* [14] The secret counsel of the LORD is for those
that fear Him,
and His covenant, that they may know it.

* [15] My eyes are ever toward the LORD,
for He will pluck my feet out of the net.
* [16] Turn to me and be gracious to me,
for I am alone and poor.

* [17] Relieve the distresses of my heart,
and bring me out of my straits.
* [18] See my affliction and my toil,
and take away all my sins.

* [19] See my enemies, that they are multiplied,
and with a violent hatred they have hated me.
* [20] Keep my soul and deliver me;
let me not be ashamed, for I have taken refuge in Thee.
* [21] May integrity and uprightness preserve me,
for I have waited for Thee.

* [22] Redeem Israel, O God,
out of all his distresses.

Psalm 26 (25)

Ju•ica me, Domine

The testimony of a good conscience

1 *A Psalm of Davi•.*

* Judge me, O LORD,
for I have walked in my integrity.
* And I have trusted in the LORD;
I will not falter.

* 2 Probe me, O LORD, and try me;
refine my reins and my heart.
* 3 For Thy mercy is before my eyes,
and I have walked in Thy truth.

* 4 I have not sat with vain men,
nor with dissemblers will I enter in.
* 5 I have hated the assembly of evildoers,
and I will not sit with the wicked.

* 6 I will wash my hands in innocence
and process around Thy altar, O LORD,
* 7 to make heard my voice in thanksgiving,
and to recount all Thy wonders.
* 8 O LORD, I have loved the habitation of Thy house,
and the place of the tabernacle of Thy glory.

* 9 Gather not my soul with sinners,
nor my life with men of blood,
* 10 in whose hands are plots,
and whose right hands are filled with bribes.

* 11 But I will walk in my integrity;
redeem me and be gracious to me.
* 12 My foot standeth on level ground;
in the assemblies I will bless the LORD.

Psalm 27 (26)

Dominus illuminatio mea

"One thing is necessary" (Luke 10:42)

1 *A Psalm of David.*

* The LORD is my light and my salvation;
whom shall I fear?
* The LORD is the stronghold of my life;
whom shall I dread?

* 2 When evildoers draw near against me,
to eat up my flesh,
* my adversaries and my enemies,
they stumble and fall.

* 3 If a camp be encamped against me,
my heart shall not fear;
* if a battle arise against me,
in this too will I be confident.

* 4 One thing have I asked of the LORD,
this will I seek:
* that I may dwell in the house of the LORD,
all the days of my life,
* to behold the delightfulness of the LORD
and to inquire in His temple.

* 5 For He will conceal me in His shelter,
in the day of evil.
* He will hide me in the secret place of His tabernacle;
He will set me high upon a rock.

* 6 And now my head shall be lifted up
above my enemies round about me.
* And I will offer in His tabernacle †
sacrifices with jubilation.
I will sing and chant a psalm to the LORD.

* 7 Hear, O LORD, my voice when I call;
be gracious to me, and answer me.
* 8 My heart hath said of Thee:
"Seek ye My face."

* Thy face, O LORD, will I seek.
9 Hide not Thy face from me;
* turn not away Thy servant in anger;
Thou hast been my help.
* Abandon me not and forsake me not,
O God of my salvation.
* 10 For my father and my mother have forsaken me,
but the LORD will take me up.

* 11 Teach me Thy way, O LORD, †
and lead me on a level path
because of my foes.
* 12 Give me not up to the will of my adversaries, †
for false witnesses have risen up against me,
and they breathe out violence.

* 13 I believe that I shall see the goodness of the LORD
in the land of the living.
* 14 Expect the LORD. †
Be strong, and let thy heart be steadfast,
and expect the LORD.

Psalm 28 (27)

Ad te, Domine

Supplications heeded

1 *A Psalm of David.*

* Unto Thee, O LORD, will I call;
my rock, be not deaf to me,
* lest if Thou be silent to me,
I become like those that go down into the pit.

* 2 Hear the voice of my supplications,
when I cry to Thee for help,
* when I lift up my hands
toward Thy innermost sanctuary.

* 3 Drag me not off with the wicked
and with the wrongdoers,
* who speak peace with their neighbours,
but evil is in their hearts.

* 4 Give to them according to their works,
and according to the evil of their deeds.
* According to the work of their hands, give to them;
render to them their recompense.
* 5 Because they understand not the deeds of the LORD, †
and the work of His hands,
He will tear them down and not build them up.

* 6 Blessed be the LORD,
for He hath heard the voice of my supplications.
* 7 The LORD is my strength and my shield;
in Him my heart hath trusted;
* and I have been helped, and my heart hath exulted,
and with my song I will give thanks to Him.

* 8 The LORD is the strength of His people,
And He is a stronghold of salvation for His anointed.
* 9 Save Thy people, and bless Thy inheritance,
and shepherd them and bear them up forever.

Psalm 29 (28)

Afferte Domino

Theophany over the waters: baptism prefigured (cf. Mark 1:9-11)

1 *A Psalm of David.*

* Ascribe to the LORD, ye sons of God,
ascribe to the LORD glory and strength.
* 2 Ascribe to the LORD the glory of His name;
adore the LORD in holy splendour.

* 3 The voice of the LORD is over the waters; †
the God of glory hath thundered;
the LORD is over many waters.
* 4 The voice of the LORD in power,
the voice of the LORD in splendour.

* 5 The voice of the LORD breaketh the cedars,
and the LORD will break the cedars of Lebanon.
* 6 And He will make Lebanon dance like a calf,
and Sirion like a young wild ox.

* 7 The voice of the LORD cleaveth flames of fire. †
8 The voice of the LORD shaketh the wilderness;
the LORD shaketh the wilderness of Kadesh.
* 9 The voice of the LORD maketh the hinds to calve †
and strippeth the forests bare,
and in His temple all say, "Glory."

* 10 The LORD sat above the flood,
and the LORD shall sit as king forever.
* 11 The LORD will give strength to His people;
the LORD will bless His people with peace.

Psalm 30 (29)

Exaltabo te, Domine

"Great joy" in the morning (Matthew 28:8)

1 *A Psalm. A song at the dedication of the temple. Of David.*

* 2 I will exalt Thee, O LORD, for Thou hast drawn me up,
and hast not let my enemies rejoice over me.

* 3 O LORD my God, I cried to Thee for help,
and Thou hast healed me.
* 4 O LORD, Thou hast brought up my soul from hell,
kept me alive from among those going down into the pit.

* 5 Sing psalms to the LORD, O ye His saints,
and give thanks to the remembrance of His holiness.
* 6 Because His anger is but for a moment,
for a lifetime His good will.
* Weeping may come to lodge in the evening,
but in the morning there shall ring out shouts of joy.

* 7 Now I had said in my security:
"I shall never be moved."
* 8 O LORD, in Thy good will,
Thou didst make me stand like a strong mountain;
* Thou didst turn away Thy face,
and I was dismayed.

* 9 To Thee, O LORD, did I cry,
and to my God I made supplication.
* 10 "What profit is there in my blood,
when I go down to corruption?
* Will dust give thanks to Thee?
Will it declare Thy truth?"

* 11 The LORD heard and was gracious to me;
the LORD became my helper.

* 12 Thou hast turned my mourning into dancing for me;
Thou hast loosed my sackcloth and girded me with gladness,
* 13 that my glory may sing psalms to Thee and not be still:
O LORD my God, I will give thanks to Thee forever.

Psalm 31 (30)

In te, Domine, speravi

"Father, into Thy hands I commend my spirit" (Luke 23:46)

1 *To the choirmaster. A Psalm of David.*

* 2 In Thee, O LORD, have I taken refuge; †
let me never be ashamed;
in Thy justice rescue me.
* 3 Incline Thy ear to me;
make haste to deliver me.

* Be a rock of refuge for me,
a fortified house to save me.
* 4 For Thou art my rock and my fortress,
and for Thy name's sake, Thou wilt lead me
and guide me.
* 5 Thou wilt bring me out of the net that they have
hidden for me,
for Thou art my refuge.

* 6 Into Thy hands I commend my spirit;
Thou hast redeemed me, O LORD, the God of truth.

* 7 I have hated them that observe worthless vanities,
but I have trusted in the LORD.
* 8 I will exult and be glad in Thy mercy, †
for Thou hast looked upon my affliction.
Thou hast known the straits of my soul,
* 9 and hast not shut me up in the hands of the enemy;
Thou hast set my feet in a broad place.

* [10] Be gracious to me, O LORD,
for I am in distress;
* my eye is wasted with grief,
my soul and my belly.
* [11] For my life is spent with sorrow,
and my years with groaning;
* my strength faileth because of my iniquity,
and my bones are wasted away.

* [12] Because of all my adversaries,
I have become a reproach,
* and especially to my neighbours,
and a dread to my acquaintances.

* Those that see me outside
flee from me.
* [13] I am forgotten from the mind as one dead;
I have become as a ruined vessel.

* [14] For I have heard the whispering of many —
terror on every side —
* as they took counsel together against me;
they plotted to take my life.

* [15] But I have trusted in Thee, O LORD;
I have said, "Thou art my God."
* [16] My times are in Thy hands; deliver me †
from the hand of my enemies
and from my persecutors.
* [17] Make Thy face shine upon Thy servant;
save me in Thy mercy.
* [18] Let me not be ashamed, O LORD,
for I have called upon Thee.
* Let the wicked be ashamed;
let them be made silent in hell.
* [19] Let lying lips be made dumb, †
which speak insolently against the just
in pride and contempt.

* [20] O how abundant is Thy goodness, O Lord,
which Thou hast laid up for those that fear Thee.
* Thou hast wrought it for those that take refuge in Thee,
in the sight of the sons of men.
* [21] Thou wilt hide them in the hiding place of Thy presence,
from the schemes of men;
* Thou wilt conceal them in Thy tabernacle
from the strife of tongues.

* [22] Blessed be the LORD, †
for He hath wonderfully shewn me His mercy
in a fortified city.

* [23] Although I had said in my alarm,
"I am cut off from before Thy eyes,"
* yet Thou didst hear the voice of my supplications,
when I cried to Thee for help.

* [24] O love the LORD, all ye His saints.
The LORD preserveth the faithful.
* But He abundantly repayeth
him that acteth proudly.

* [25] Be strong, and let your heart be steadfast,
all ye that hope in the LORD.

Psalm 32 (31)

Beati quorum

Confession and forgiveness

(Second Penitential Psalm)

1 *Of David. A Maskil.*

* Blessed is he whose transgression is taken away,
whose sin is covered.
* 2 Blessed is the man to whom the LORD †
imputeth no iniquity,
and in whose spirit there is no guile.

* 3 When I kept silent, my bones wasted away,
while I roared all day long.
* 4 For night and day Thy hand
was heavy upon me;
* my sap was changed
into the droughts of summer. *Selah*

* 5 I made known my sin to Thee,
and my iniquity I did not cover up.
* I said, "I will confess against myself
my transgression to the LORD."
* And Thou didst take away
the iniquity of my sin. *Selah*

* 6 Therefore shall every pious man pray to Thee
at an opportune time.
* Even in a flood of many waters,
they shall not reach to him.
* 7 Thou art a hiding place for me: †
Thou wilt preserve me from distress;
Thou wilt surround me with ringing cries of
deliverance. *Selah*

* 8 "I will give thee insight and instruct thee
in the way that thou shalt go;

*   I will counsel thee,
My eye being upon thee.
* 9 Be not like a horse or a mule,
without understanding,
*   which must be curbed with bit and bridle,
or they will not draw near to thee."

* 10 Many are the sorrows of the wicked; †
but he that trusteth in the LORD,
mercy shall surround him.

* 11 Be glad in the LORD,
and exult, ye just.
*   And ring out your joy,
all ye upright of heart.

Psalm 33 (32)

Exultate, justi

The divine mercy (ḥeseḏ) in creation and in history

* 1 Ring out your joy in the LORD, O ye just.
Praise becometh the upright.

* 2 Give thanks to the LORD upon the harp;
with a psaltery of ten strings chant a psalm to Him.
* 3 Sing to Him a new song;
play skillfully, with jubilation.
* 4 For the word of the LORD is upright,
and all His works are done in faithfulness.
* 5 He loveth justice and judgment.
The earth is full of the mercy of the LORD.

* 6 By the word of the LORD were the heavens made,
and by the Spirit of His mouth all their host.
* 7 He gathered the waters of the sea as in a heap;
He put the deeps into storehouses.

* 8 Let all the earth fear the LORD;
let all the inhabitants of the world be in awe of Him.
* 9 For He spoke, and it came to be;
He commanded, and it stood forth.

* 10 The LORD smasheth the counsel of the Gentiles;
He disalloweth the designs of the peoples.
* 11 But the counsel of the LORD shall stand forever,
the designs of His heart from generation to generation.

* 12 Blessed the nation whose God is the LORD,
the people whom He hath chosen for His inheritance.
* 13 The LORD hath looked from heaven;
He hath seen all the children of men.
* 14 From the place of His habitation He hath gazed
upon all the inhabitants of the earth,
* 15 He Who formeth their hearts one and all,
Who understandeth all their works.

* 16 A king is not saved by a multitude of forces;
a mighty man is not delivered by abundant strength.
* 17 The horse is a deception for salvation;
despite its great force, it cannot give escape.

* 18 Behold, the eye of the LORD is upon those that fear Him,
upon those that hope in His mercy,
* 19 to deliver their soul from death,
and to keep them alive in famine.

* 20 Our soul hath waited for the LORD;
He is our help and our shield.
* 21 For in Him doth our heart rejoice,
for in His holy name have we trusted.

* 22 Let Thy mercy, O LORD, be upon us,
even as we have hoped in Thee.

Psalm 34 (33)

Bene•icam Dominum

Beginners (*depart*), proficients (*do good*), and advanced (*seek peace*)

(cf. St. Thomas Aquinas, Summa Theologiae, II - II, q. 24, a.9)

1 *A Psalm of Davi•, when he feigne• ma•ness before Abimelech an•, •riven out by him, he went away.*

* 2 I will bless the LORD at all times;
His praise shall continually be in my mouth.
* 3 In the LORD shall my soul boast;
let the meek hear and be glad.

* 4 O magnify the LORD with me,
and let us exalt His name together.
* 5 I sought the LORD, and He answered me,
and delivered me from all my fears.

* 6 Look to Him and be enlightened,
and your faces shall not be confounded.
* 7 This poor man called, and the LORD heard him,
and saved him out of all his troubles.

* 8 The angel of the LORD encampeth
around those that fear Him and delivereth them.
* 9 Taste and see that the LORD is good;
blessed the man who taketh refuge in Him.

* 10 Fear the LORD, ye His saints,
for nothing is wanting to those that fear Him.
* 11 The young lions lack and go hungry,
but those that seek the LORD want for no good thing.

* 12 Come, children, hearken to me;
I will teach you the fear of the LORD.
* 13 Who is the man who would have life,
who loveth days for seeing good?

* 14 Preserve thy tongue from evil,
and thy lips from speaking deceit.
* 15 Depart from evil and do good;
seek peace and pursue it.

* 16 The eyes of the LORD are upon the just,
and His ears toward their cry for help.
* 17 The face of the LORD is against evildoers,
to cut off the remembrance of them from the earth.

* 18 They cried out and the LORD heard,
and out of all their straits He delivered them.
* 19 The LORD is nigh unto the brokenhearted,
and will save the humbled in spirit.

* 20 Many are the evils of the just,
but out of them all the LORD will deliver him.
* 21 He keepeth all his bones;
not one of them shall be broken.

* 22 Evil shall slay the wicked,
and those that hate the just shall be guilty.
* 23 The LORD redeemeth the souls of His servants,
and none shall be guilty that take refuge in Him.

Psalm 35 (34)

Ju•ica, Domine

"The Lord ... willeth the peace of His servant"

1 *A Psalm of Davi•.*

* Contend, O LORD, with those that contend with me;
fight against those that fight against me.
* 2 Take hold of shield and buckler,
and rise up for my help.
* 3 Draw the spear and shut up the way
against my pursuers.
* Say unto my soul:
"I am thy salvation."

* 4 Let them be ashamed and disgraced
that seek my soul.
* Let them be turned back and confounded
that devise evil against me.
* 5 Let them be like chaff before the wind,
with the angel of the LORD driving them on.
* 6 Let their way be dark and slippery,
with the angel of the LORD pursuing them.

* 7 For without cause they hid their net for me,
without cause they dug a pit for my soul.
* 8 Let ruin come upon him unawares, †
and his own net, which he hid, catch him;
let him fall into that very ruin.

* 9 But my soul shall exult in the LORD;
it shall rejoice in His salvation.
* 10 All my bones shall say,
"O LORD, Who is like Thee:
* who deliverest the poor from him too strong for him,
and the poor and the needy from him that despoileth him?"

* 11 Violent witnesses rise up;
they ask me of things I know not.
* 12 They repay me evil for good,
bereavement for my soul.

* 13 But I, when they were sick, wore sackcloth; †
I humbled my soul with fasting,
and my prayer would return to my bosom.
* 14 As if for a friend or for my brother I went about, †
as one mourning a mother,
bowed down in gloom.

* 15 But when I stumbled, †
they rejoiced and gathered together;
they gathered together against me.
* Assailants I did not know
tore at me and would not be still,
* 16 like godless mockers at a feast,
gnashing at me with their teeth.

* 17 O LORD, how long wilt Thou look on? †
Restore my soul from their malice,
my lonely self from the lions.
* 18 I will give thanks to Thee in the great church;
amidst a numerous people, I will praise Thee.

* 19 Let not my false enemies
rejoice over me,
* nor let those that hate me without cause
wink the eye.

* 20 For they speak not peace, †
but against those that are quiet in the land,
they devise words of deceit.
* 21 And they opened wide their mouths against me; †
they said, "Aha, aha,
our eyes have seen it."

* [22] Thou hast seen: O LORD, keep not silent.
O LORD, be not far from me.
* [23] Rouse Thyself and awake for my judgment,
for my cause, O my God and my Lord.

* [24] Judge me according to Thy justice, †
O LORD my God,
and let them not rejoice over me.
* [25] Let them not say in their hearts,
"Well done for our souls,"
* nor let them say,
"We have swallowed him up."

* [26] Let them be ashamed and confounded together
that rejoice at my evil.
* Let them be clothed with shame and disgrace
that magnify themselves against me.

* [27] Let those that will my justice
cry aloud and rejoice,
* and let them say continually, "The LORD be magnified,
Who willeth the peace of His servant."
* [28] And my tongue shall meditate Thy justice,
Thy praise all the day.

Psalm 36 (35)

Dixit injustus

The malice of the wicked and the mercy of God

1 *To the choirmaster. Of Davi•, the servant of the* LORD.

* 2 Transgression speaketh to the wicked
in the midst of his heart;
* there is no fear of God
before his eyes.

* 3 For he flattereth himself in his own eyes,
that his iniquity may not be found out and hated.
* 4 The words of his mouth are wrong and deceit;
he hath ceased to perceive that he might do good.
* 5 He deviseth wrong on his bed; †
he setteth himself on a way that is not good;
he rejecteth not evil.

* 6 O LORD, Thy mercy is in the heavens;
Thy faithfulness is unto the clouds.
* 7 Thy justice is like the mountains of God; †
Thy judgments are a great deep.
Man and beast Thou wilt save, O LORD.

* 8 How precious is Thy mercy, O God! †
Therefore the children of men
shall take refuge in the shadow of Thy wings.
* 9 They shall be sated with the fatness of Thy house,
and Thou shalt give them drink from the stream of
Thy pleasures.
* 10 For with Thee is the fountain of life,
and in Thy light shall we see light.

* 11 Prolong Thy mercy to those that know Thee,
and Thy justice for the upright of heart.
* 12 Let not the foot of pride overtake me,
nor the hand of the wicked displace me.
* 13 There have the wrongdoers fallen;
they are thrust down, and cannot arise.

Psalm 37 (36)

Noli aemulari

"The meek shall inherit the earth" (Matthew 5:5)

1 *A Psalm of Davi•.*

* Be not enraged at the evildoers,
nor envy those that do wrong,
* 2 for they shall soon wither like the grass,
and fade like the green herb.

* 3 Trust in the LORD and do good;
dwell in the land and feed in faithfulness.
* 4 And take delight in the LORD,
and He will give thee the requests of thy heart.

* 5 Commit thy way to the LORD,
and trust in Him, and He will do it;
* 6 and He will bring forth thy justice as the light,
and thy judgment as the noonday.

* 7 Be still before the LORD and wait for Him; †
be not enraged at one who prospereth in his way,
at a man who carrieth out plots.

* 8 Desist from anger and forsake wrath;
be not enraged, so as only to bring evil.
* 9 For evildoers shall be cut off; †
but they that wait for the LORD,
they shall inherit the land.

* 10 Yet a little while, and the wicked shall not be;
if thou markest well his place, he shall not be there.
* 11 But the meek shall inherit the land,
and take delight in abundant peace.

* 12 The wicked plotteth against the just
and gnasheth his teeth at him.
* 13 But the LORD will laugh at him,
for He hath seen that his day is coming.

* [14] The wicked have drawn the sword and bent their bow †
to fell the poor and the needy,
to slay those whose way is upright.
* [15] Their sword shall enter into their own heart,
and their bows shall be broken.

* [16] Better is a little to the just
than the abundance of many wicked.
* [17] For the arms of the wicked shall be broken,
but the LORD upholdeth the just.

* [18] The LORD knoweth the days of the blameless,
and their inheritance shall be forever.
* [19] They shall not be ashamed in time of evil,
and in days of famine they shall be satisfied.

* [20] For the wicked shall perish,
and the enemies of the LORD,
* like the splendour of the meadows vanish;
they vanish like smoke.

* [21] The wicked borroweth and will not repay,
but the just is gracious and giveth.
* [22] For those blessed by Him shall inherit the land,
but those cursed by Him shall be cut off.

* [23] From the LORD are the steps of a man established,
and he delighteth in His way.
* [24] Though he fall, he shall not be cast headlong,
for the LORD upholdeth his hand.

* [25] I have been young, and now am I old, †
and I have not seen the just forsaken,
nor his seed begging bread.
* [26] All the day he is gracious and lendeth,
and his seed become a blessing.

* [27] Depart from evil and do good,
and so abide forever.
* [28] For the LORD loveth judgment,
and He will not forsake His saints.

* The unjust shall be wiped out forever,
and the seed of the wicked cut off.
* 29 The just shall inherit the land,
and dwell upon it forever.

* 30 The mouth of the just shall meditate wisdom,
and his tongue shall speak judgment.
* 31 The law of his God is in his heart,
and his steps do not falter.

* 32 The wicked watcheth for the just
and seeketh to put him to death.
* 33 The LORD will not leave him in his hands,
nor have him condemned when he is judged.

* 34 Expect the LORD, and keep His way, †
and He will exalt thee to inherit the land;
when the wicked are cut off, thou shalt see it.

* 35 I have seen the wicked overbearing,
and towering like the cedars of Lebanon.
* 36 And I passed by, and lo, he was not;
and I sought him, but he could not be found.

* 37 Observe integrity and behold uprightness,
for there is a future for the man of peace.
* 38 But transgressors shall be done away with together;
the future of the wicked shall be cut off.

* 39 The salvation of the just is from the LORD;
He is their stronghold in the time of trouble.
* 40 And the LORD will help them and deliver them; †
He will deliver them from the wicked and save them,
because they have taken refuge in Him.

Psalm 38 (37)

Domine, ne in furore

"All my desire is before Thee"

(Third Penitential Psalm)

1 *A Psalm of David. For a commemoration.*

* 2 O LORD, rebuke me not in Thy fury,
nor discipline me in Thy wrath,
* 3 for Thy arrows have penetrated me,
and Thy hand hath come down upon me.

* 4 There is no soundness in my flesh
because of Thy indignation;
* there is no peace in my bones
because of my sins.

* 5 For my iniquities have gone over my head,
and like a heavy burden, they are too heavy for me.
* 6 My wounds are putrid and festering
because of my folly.
* 7 I am utterly bent and bowed down;
I go about gloomy all the day.

* 8 For my loins are filled with burning,
and there is no soundness in my flesh.
* 9 I am utterly numbed and crushed;
I roar because of the groaning of my heart.

* 10 O Lord, all my desire is before Thee;
my groaning is not hidden from Thee.
* 11 My heart throbbeth, my strength hath forsaken me,
and even the light of my eyes is not with me.

* 12 My friends and my neighbours †
stand aloof from my plague,
and my near of kin have stood afar off.

* [13] And those that seek my soul have laid snares, †
and those that seek my evil have spoken of ruin,
and meditate treachery all the day long.

* [14] But I am like the deaf, I hear not,
and like the dumb, who openeth not his mouth;
* [15] and I am as a man who heareth not,
and in whose mouth are no rebukes.

* [16] For in Thee, O LORD, have I hoped;
Thou wilt answer, O LORD my God.
* [17] For I have said, "Lest they rejoice over me, †
who when my foot slippeth,
magnify themselves against me."

* [18] For I am ready to stumble,
and my pain is continually before me.
* [19] For I declare my iniquity,
and I am anxious because of my sin.

* [20] But my enemies live on and are strong,
and those that hate me wrongfully are multiplied.
* [21] And those that repay evil for good
accuse me because I pursue good.

* [22] Forsake me not, O LORD.
O my God, be not far from me.
* [23] Make haste to help me,
O Lord, my salvation.

Psalm 39 (38)

Dixi custo•iam

Hoping in the First Cause of all

1 *To the choirmaster, Je•uthun. A Psalm of Davi•.*

* 2 I said, “I will keep my ways,
that I sin not with my tongue;
* I will put a muzzle on my mouth,
as long as the wicked is before me.”
* 3 I was dumb, keeping still;
I was silent, even from good.

* But my grief was stirred;
4 my heart grew hot within me.
* In my meditation, a fire was kindled;
5 I spoke with my tongue:
* “O LORD, make me know my end, †
and what is the measure of my days,
that I may know how fleeting I am.”

* 6 Behold Thou hast made my days as handbreadths,
and my lifetime is as nothing before Thee.
* Surely every man standing is but vanity. *Selah*
7 Surely man goeth about as a shadow.
* Surely he is disquieted in vain;
he heapeth up, and knoweth not who will gather.

* 8 And now, O Lord, what is my expectation?
My hope is in Thee.
* 9 Deliver me from all my transgressions;
make me not the reproach of the fool.
* 10 I am dumb, I open not my mouth,
because Thou hast done it.

* 11 Remove Thy scourge from me;
I perish from the blows of Thy hand.

* 12 Thou dost discipline a man with rebukes for iniquity †
and consume, like a moth, what he desireth.
Surely every man is vanity. *Selah*

* 13 Hear my prayer, O LORD, †
and give ear to my cry for help;
be not deaf to my tears.
* For I am a stranger with Thee,
a sojourner like all my fathers.
* 14 Look away from me, that I may be relieved,
before I depart and be no more.

Psalm 40 (39)

Expectans expectavi

The sacrifice of oneself (Hebrews 10:1-10)

1 *To the choirmaster. A Psalm of Davi•.*

* 2 With expectation I awaited the LORD, †
and He inclined unto me
3 and heard my cry for help.

* And He brought me up out of the tumultuous pit,
out of the miry clay,
* and He set my feet upon a rock;
He made my footsteps firm.
* 4 And He put a new song into my mouth,
a hymn of praise to our God.
* Many shall see and shall fear,
and shall trust in the LORD.

* 5 Blessed is the man who hath made
the LORD his trust
* and hath not turned to the proud,
and those who turn away to falsehood.

* [6] Thou hast multiplied, O LORD my God,
Thy wondrous works,
* and Thy designs regarding us:
there is none to compare with Thee.
* Were I to declare and to speak of them,
they would be more than can be numbered.

* [7] Sacrifice and offering Thou didst not wish,
but a body Thou didst prepare for me.
* Burnt offering and sin offering Thou didst not require. †
[8] Then said I, "Behold, I have come.
In the roll of the book it is written of me.
* [9] To do Thy will, O my God, I have desired,
and Thy law is within my inmost parts."

* [10] I announced the good tidings of justice
in the great church;
* lo, I did not restrain my lips,
as Thou knowest, O LORD.
* [11] I have not hidden Thy justice within my heart;
I have spoken of Thy faithfulness and Thy salvation.
* I have not concealed Thy mercy and Thy truth
from the great church.

* [12] Withhold not Thou, O LORD,
Thy compassion from me;
* may Thy mercy and Thy truth
continually preserve me.
* [13] For evils have encompassed me
which are without number;
* my iniquities have overtaken me,
and I cannot see.
* They are more numerous than the hairs of my head,
and my heart hath forsaken me.

* [14] Be pleased, O LORD, to deliver me;
O LORD, make haste to help me.
* [15] Let them be ashamed and confounded together
that seek to snatch away my soul.

* Let them be turned back and disgraced
that wish me evil.
* 16 Let them be appalled because of their shame
that say to me, "Aha, aha."

* 17 Let all that seek Thee
rejoice and be glad in Thee,
* and let those that love Thy salvation
say always, "The LORD be magnified."

* 18 Although I am poor and needy,
the Lord will take thought of me.
* Thou art my help and my deliverer:
O my God, make no delay.

Psalm 41 (40)

Beatus qui intelligit

"He who ate my bread has lifted up his heel against me"
(John 13:18b)

1 *To the choirmaster. A Psalm of David.*

* 2 Blessed is he who considereth the weak;
the LORD will deliver him in the evil day.
* 3 The LORD will keep him and give him life, †
and will make him blessed in the land,
and will not give him up to the will of his enemies.
* 4 The LORD will sustain him on his sickbed;
Thou wilt restore him from his bed in his every illness.

* 5 I said: "O LORD, be gracious to me;
heal my soul, for I have sinned against Thee."
* 6 My enemies speak evil of me:
"When will he die and his name perish?"
* 7 And if one come in to see me he speaketh vain things; †
his heart gathereth mischief to itself;
he goeth out and telleth it abroad.

* [8] All that hate me whisper together against me;
against me they devise evil for me.
* [9] "A devilish thing is poured out upon him,
and he that lieth there will rise up no more."
* [10] Even the man of my peace, in whom I trusted, †
who ate my bread,
hath lifted up his heel against me.

* [11] But Thou, O LORD, be gracious to me,
and raise me up, that I may requite them.
* [12] By this I know that Thou hast good will toward me:
that my enemy shall not shout in exultation over me;
* [13] but Thou hast upheld me in my integrity,
and made me stand in Thy sight forever.

* [14] Blessed be the LORD, the God of Israel,
from everlasting and unto everlasting. Amen, amen.

BOOK II

Psalms 42-72

(The king•om of Davi•)

Psalm 42 (41)

Quema•mo•um •esi•erat cervus

Yearning for communion with God in His temple

1 *To the choirmaster. A Maskil of the Sons of Korah.*

* 2 As the hart panteth
after the watercourses,
* so my soul panteth
after Thee, O God.

* 3 My soul is thirsting for God,
for the living God;
* when shall I enter and appear
before the face of God?

* 4 My tears have been my bread
day and night,
* while they say to me all the day long:
"Where is thy God?"

* 5 These things do I remember,
and pour out my soul within me:
* how I used to cross over, †
processing with the throng,
up to the house of God,

*   amid the sound of joyous cries and thanksgiving,
      a multitude celebrating the festival.

* [6] Why art thou cast down, O my soul,
      and why art thou disquieted within me?
*   Hope in God, for I will again confess to Him,
      the salvation of my countenance and my God.

* [7] My soul is cast down within me,
      therefore will I remember Thee
*   from the land of Jordan and the Hermon range,
      from Mount Mizar.
* [8] Deep calleth unto deep
      at the voice of Thy cataracts;
*   all Thy breakers and Thy waves
      have passed over me.

* [9] By day the LORD will command His mercy, †
      and by night His song is with me,
      a prayer to the God of my life.

* [10] I will say to God: "Thou art my rock.
      Why hast Thou forgotten me?
*   And why do I go about gloomy
      under the oppression of the enemy?"
* [11] While there is a crushing in my bones,
      my adversaries reproach me,
*   as they say to me all the day long:
      "Where is thy God?"

* [12] Why art thou cast down, O my soul,
      and why art thou disquieted within me?
*   Hope in God, for I will again confess to Him,
      the salvation of my countenance and my God.

Psalm 43 (42)

Ju• ica me, Deus

The joy of liturgical confession at God's altar

* 1 Judge me, O God, and plead my cause
against a nation without mercy;
* from the deceitful and unjust man
deliver Thou me.

* 2 For Thou, O God, art my strength.
Why hast Thou cast me off?
* Why do I go about gloomy
under the oppression of the enemy?

* 3 Send forth Thy light and Thy truth;
let them lead me;
* let them bring me to Thy holy hill
and to Thy tabernacles.

* 4 And I will go in to the altar of God,
to God, my exultant joy.
* And I will confess to Thee upon the harp,
O God, my God.

* 5 Why art thou cast down, O my soul,
and why art thou disquieted within me?
* Hope in God, for I will again confess to Him,
the salvation of my countenance and my God.

Psalm 44 (43)

Deus, auribus nostris

The enigma of innocent suffering (cf. Romans 8:36)

1 *To the choirmaster. A Maskil of the Sons of Korah.*

* 2 O God, we have heard with our ears,
our fathers have told us,
* of the deed Thou didst in their days,
in the days of old.

* 3 Thou with Thy hand didst dispossess the nations,
but them Thou didst plant;
* Thou didst afflict the peoples,
but them Thou didst spread abroad.

* 4 For not by their own sword did they possess the land,
nor did their own arm save them,
* but Thy right hand and Thy arm †
and the light of Thy countenance,
for Thou wast well pleased with them.

* 5 Thou art my king and my God,
Who commandest the salvation of Jacob.
* 6 In Thee do we push back our adversaries,
and in Thy name do we trample down our assailants.

* 7 For I will not trust in my bow,
nor shall my sword save me.
* 8 For Thou hast saved us from our adversaries,
and shamed those that hate us.
* 9 In God have we boasted all the day,
and we will acclaim Thy name forever. *Selah*

* 10 Yet Thou hast cast us off and disgraced us,
and Thou goest not forth with our armies.
* 11 Thou makest us turn back from the adversary,
and those that hate us have plundered us at will.

* 12 Thou givest us like sheep to be eaten,
and hast scattered us among the nations.
* 13 Thou sellest Thy people for a trifle,
and hast gained nothing from their price.

* 14 Thou makest us a reproach to our neighbours,
a mockery and a derision to those around us.
* 15 Thou makest us a byword among the nations,
a shaking of the head among the peoples.

* 16 All the day my disgrace is before me,
and the shame of my face hath covered me,
* 17 at the voice of the reproacher and blasphemer,
at the face of the enemy and avenger.

* 18 All this hath come upon us, though we have not
forgotten Thee,
nor have we been false to Thy covenant;
* 19 our heart hath not turned back,
nor have our steps declined from Thy path.
* 20 Yet Thou hast crushed us in a place of jackals,
and covered us with the shadow of death.

* 21 If we had forgotten the name of our God,
and spread forth our hands to a strange god,
* 22 would not God search this out?
For He knoweth the secrets of the heart.
* 23 Yet for Thy sake we are killed all day long;
we are counted as sheep for the slaughter.

* 24 Awake, why sleepest Thou, O Lord?
Arise, do not cast us off forever.
* 25 Why dost Thou turn away Thy face,
and forget our affliction and oppression?

* 26 For our soul is bowed down to the dust;
our belly cleaveth to the earth.
* Rise up for our help,
and redeem us for the sake of Thy mercy.

Psalm 45 (44)

Eructavit cor meum

"My beloved to me, and I to him" (Canticle of Canticles 2:16)

1 *To the choirmaster. Accor•ing to Lilies.*
Of the Sons of Korah. Maskil. A love song.

* 2 My heart is stirred with a good word. †
I speak my work to the king.
My tongue is the pen of a ready scribe.

* 3 Thou art the fairest of the sons of men; †
grace is poured out upon thy lips;
therefore God hath blessed thee forever.

* 4 Gird thy sword upon thy thigh, O mighty One,
in thy majesty and thy splendour.
* 5 And in thy splendour, prosper, ride on, †
because of truth and meekness and justice.
And let thy right hand teach thee terrible deeds.
* 6 Thy arrows are sharp — †
as peoples fall under thee —
in the hearts of the king's enemies.

* 7 Thy throne, O God, is forever and ever;
a scepter of equity is the scepter of thy kingdom.
* 8 Thou hast loved justice and hated wickedness; †
therefore God, thy God, hath anointed thee,
with the oil of gladness above thy fellows.

* 9 Thy garments are all myrrh and aloes and cassia;
from ivory palaces stringed instruments gladden thee.
* 10 Daughters of kings are among thy precious ones;
the queen standeth at thy right hand in gold of Ophir.

* 11 Hear, O daughter, and see, and incline thy ear,
and forget thy people and thy father's house;
* 12 and the king shall greatly desire thy beauty;
since he is thy Lord, worship thou him.

* [13] And the daughter of Tyre shall come with gifts;
the richest of the people shall entreat thy face.

* [14] All glorious is the king's daughter within;
her clothing is threaded with gold.
* [15] In many-coloured robes, she shall be brought to the king;
after her the virgins, her companions, shall be
brought to thee.
* [16] They shall be brought along with joy and exultation;
they shall enter into the palace of the king.

* [17] Instead of thy fathers shall be thy sons;
thou shalt make them princes over all the earth.
* [18] I will make thy name remembered throughout
all generations;
therefore shall the peoples acclaim thee forever and ever.

Psalm 46 (45)

Deus noster refugium

Easter: "God will help her at the break of the morning"
(St. Basil)

[1] *To the choirmaster. Of the Sons of Korah. Accor•ing to "Virgins..."*
A Song.

* [2] God is our refuge and strength,
found to be a great help in times of distress.
* [3] Therefore we will not fear though the earth
should change,
and the mountains be moved into the heart of the sea;
* [4] even though its waters roar and foam,
even though the mountains quake at its surging. *Selah*

* [5] There is a river — the streams thereof †
make glad the city of God,
the holy tabernacles of the Most High.

* 6 God is in the midst of her, she shall not be moved;
God will help her at the break of the morning.
* 7 The Gentiles roared, kingdoms were moved;
He uttered His voice, the earth melted.

* 8 The LORD of hosts is with us;
our high place is the God of Jacob. *Selah*

* 9 Come, behold the works of the LORD, †
what desolations He hath done on the earth.
He maketh wars to cease to the end of the earth;
* 10 He breaketh the bow and shattereth the spear;
He burneth the shields with fire.
* 11 "Desist, and know that I am God:
I will be exalted among the Gentiles, I will be exalted in the earth."

* 12 The LORD of hosts is with us;
our high place is the God of Jacob. *Selah*

Psalm 47 (46)

Omnes gentes, plau• ite

Ascension and enthronement (cf. Mark 16:19)

1 *To the choirmaster. Of the Sons of Korah. A Psalm.*

* 2 All peoples, clap your hands;
make jubilation to God with exultant voice;
* 3 for the LORD, the Most High, is to be feared,
a great king over all the earth.

* 4 He subdued peoples under us,
and nations under our feet.
* 5 He chose our inheritance for us,
the pride of Jacob, whom He loveth. *Selah*

* [6] God is ascended with jubilation,
the LORD with the sound of the horn.
* [7] Sing a psalm to God, sing a psalm;
sing a psalm to our king, sing a psalm.

* [8] For God is king of all the earth;
sing a psalm insightfully.
* [9] God reigneth over the nations;
God sitteth on His holy throne.

* [10] The princes of the peoples are gathered together
with the people of the God of Abraham.
* For the shields of the earth belong to God;
He is exceedingly exalted.

Psalm 48 (47)

Magnus Dominus

The "invincible stability" of the city of God

(First Vatican Council , Denzinger 1974/3013)

[1] *A Song. A Psalm. Of the Sons of Korah.*

* [2] The LORD is great and exceedingly to be praised
in the city of our God.
* [3] His holy mountain, fair in elevation,
is the joy of all the earth.

* Mount Zion, in the recesses of the north,
is the city of the great king.
* [4] God in her fortified palaces
is known as a height of refuge.

* [5] For lo, the kings were assembled;
they passed along together.
* [6] They saw it; at once they were astounded,
they were dismayed, they hastened off in fear.

* 7 Trembling took hold of them there,
pangs like a woman in labour.
* 8 By the east wind Thou shatterest
the ships of Tarshish.

* 9 As we have heard, so we have seen
in the city of the LORD of hosts.
* In the city of our God;
God will establish it forever. *Selah*

* 10 We have pondered Thy mercy, O God,
in the midst of Thy temple.
* 11 As is Thy name, O God,
so is Thy praise unto the ends of the earth.

* Thy right hand is full of justice;
12 let Mount Zion be glad.
* And let the daughters of Judah exult,
because of Thy judgments.

* 13 Go around Zion and make the circle about her,
count up her towers,
* 14 set your heart on her ramparts,
go through her fortified palaces;
* that you may tell the coming generation
15 that this is God.
* Our God forever and ever:
He will guide us forevermore.

Psalm 49 (48)

Au•ite haec, omnes gentes

Memento mori

(Remember thou shalt die)

1 *To the choirmaster. Of the Sons of Korah. A Psalm.*

* 2 Hear this, all ye peoples;
give ear, all ye inhabitants of the world,
* 3 both commoners and noblemen,
rich and poor together.

* 4 My mouth shall speak wisdom,
and the meditation of my heart shall be understanding.
* 5 I will incline my ear to a parable;
I will open up my riddle upon the harp.

* 6 Why should I fear in days of evil,
when the iniquity at my heels shall surround me?
* 7 Those that trust in their wealth
and boast in the multitude of their riches.

* 8 Surely no man can redeem himself;
he cannot give his atonement to God.
* 9 The redemption of his soul is precious,
and forever deficient,
* 10 that he should live on perpetually
and not see destruction.

* 11 For he shall see that the wise die; †
the fool and the brutish alike perish,
and leave their wealth to others.
* 12 Their graves are their homes forever, †
their dwelling places from generation to generation,
though they had called their lands by their names.

* 13 So man will not abide in honour;
he is like the beasts that perish.

* [14] This is the way of the self-confident,
and the end of those pleased with their own mouth. *Selah*
* [15] Like sheep they are put into hell; †
death shall shepherd them,
and the upright shall rule over them in the morning.
* And their form shall waste away;
hell shall be their habitation.

* [16] But God will redeem my soul
from the hand of hell, for He will receive me. *Selah*

* [17] Fear not when a man groweth rich,
when the glory of his house is multiplied,
* [18] for when he die, he shall not take it all,
nor shall his glory descend after him.

* [19] Though he blessed his soul while he lived,
and men will praise thee when thou doest well for thyself,
* [20] yet he shall go to the generation of his fathers,
who shall not see the light forever.

* [21] Man, when he is in honour, understandeth not;
he is like the beasts that perish.

Psalm 50 (49)

Deus deorum

The Eucharist, the Christian thank-offering

(cf. Lk 22:19-26, 1 Cor 11:23-25; Ratzinger, *Coll. Works* 11:314-318)

[1] *A Psalm of Asaph.*

* The God of gods, the LORD, †
hath spoken and called to the earth
from the rising of the sun to its setting.
* [2] Out of Zion, the perfection of beauty, God hath shone forth.
[3] Our God will come and will not keep silent.

* Before Him is a devouring fire,
and around Him it is very tempestuous.
* [4] He will call to the heavens above
and to the earth, to judge His people.

* [5] "Gather unto Me My saints,
who made a covenant with Me by sacrifice."
* [6] And the heavens shall declare His justice,
because God Himself is judge. *Selah*

* [7] "Hear, O My people, and I will speak, †
O Israel, and I will testify against thee.
God, thy God, am I.

* [8] I will not rebuke thee for thy sacrifices,
and thy burnt offerings are continually before Me.
* [9] I will accept no bullock from thy house,
nor billy goats from thy folds.

* [10] For all the beasts of the forest are Mine,
the cattle on a thousand hills.
* [11] I know all the birds of heaven,
and what moveth in the field is Mine.

* [12] If I were hungry, I would not tell thee,
for the world is Mine, and the fulness thereof.

* [13] Shall I eat the flesh of bulls,
or drink the blood of goats?

* [14] Sacrifice the thank-offering to God,
and pay thy vows to the Most High;
* [15] and call upon Me in the day of trouble:
I will deliver thee, and thou shalt glorify Me."

* [16] But to the wicked, God hath said: †
"Why dost thou recite My statutes,
and take up My covenant with thy mouth?
* [17] For thou hast hated discipline,
and cast My words behind thee.

* [18] If thou sawest a thief, thou didst run with him,
and with adulterers was thy portion.
* [19] Thou didst let loose thy mouth for evil,
and thy tongue framed deceit.
* [20] Sitting, thou didst speak against thy brother,
and give fault against thy mother's son.

* [21] These things thou didst, and I was silent. †
Thou didst suppose that I am just like thee.
I will rebuke thee, and set them in order before thy eyes.

* [22] Understand this, then, you that forget God,
lest I rend, and there be none to deliver.
* [23] He that sacrificeth the thank-offering shall glorify Me, †
and to him who setteth his way aright,
I will shew the salvation of God."

Psalm 51 (50)

Miserere mei, Deus

Contrition and the cleansing of personal and original sin

(Fourth Penitential Psalm)

1 *To the choirmaster. A Psalm of Davi•,*
2 *when Nathan the prophet came to him, after he ha• gone in to Bathsheba.*

* 3 Be gracious to me, O God, according to Thy mercy;
according to the multitude of Thy compassions,
blot out my transgression.
* 4 Wash me yet more from my iniquity,
and cleanse me from my sin.

* 5 For I know my transgression,
and my sin is ever before me.
* 6 Against Thee, Thee only, have I sinned,
and done what is evil in Thy sight,
* so that Thou mayest be justified in Thy words,
and pure in Thy judgment.
* 7 Behold, I was brought to birth in iniquity,
and in sin did my mother conceive me.

* 8 Behold, Thou desirest truth in the inmost parts,
and in secret Thou shalt teach me wisdom.
* 9 Purge me with hyssop, and I shall be cleansed;
wash me, and I shall be whiter than snow.

* 10 Make me hear joy and gladness,
that the bones that Thou hast crushed may exult.
* 11 Turn away Thy face from my sins,
and blot out all my iniquities.

* 12 A clean heart create in me, O God,
and renew a steadfast spirit within me.
* 13 Cast me not away from Thy face,
and take not Thy Holy Spirit from me.

* [14] Restore to me the joy of Thy salvation,
and uphold me with a noble spirit.
* [15] I will teach transgressors Thy ways,
and sinners shall return to Thee.

* [16] Deliver me from bloodguilt, †
O God, the God of my salvation,
and my tongue shall ring out Thy justice.
* [17] O Lord, open my lips,
and my mouth shall declare Thy praise.

* [18] For Thou wilt not delight in sacrifice, or I would give it;
with a burnt offering Thou wilt not be pleased.
* [19] A sacrifice to God is a broken spirit; †
a broken and humbled heart,
O God, Thou wilt not despise.

* [20] Do good to Zion in Thy good pleasure;
build up the walls of Jerusalem.
* [21] Then wilt Thou delight in just sacrifices, †
in burnt offerings and holocausts;
then will they offer bullocks upon Thy altar.

Psalm 52 (51)

Qui• gloriaris

"You shall laugh" (Luke 6:21)

1 *To the choirmaster. Maskil. Of Davi•,*
2 *when Doeg the E•omite came an• tol• Saul:*
"Davi• has come to the house of Abimelech."

* 3 Why dost thou boast of evil,
O man mighty by the mercy of God?
* 4 All the day thou devisest ruin; †
thy tongue is like a sharp razor,
O worker of deceit.

* 5 Thou hast loved evil more than good,
lying more than just speech. *Selah*
* 6 Thou hast loved all words that devour,
O deceitful tongue.

* 7 Therefore God will break thee down forever; †
He will snatch thee up and tear thee from thy tent,
and uproot thee from the land of the living. *Selah*

* 8 The just shall see and fear,
and they shall laugh at it:
* 9 "Behold the man
who made not God his stronghold,
* but trusted in the multitude of his riches,
and prevailed by wreaking ruin."

* 10 But I am like a luxuriant olive tree
in the house of God.
* I trust in the mercy of God
forever and ever.

* 11 I will give thanks to Thee forever,
because Thou hast done it,
* and I will await Thy name, for it is good,
in the presence of Thy saints.

Psalm 53 (52)

Dixit insipiens

The besiegers of God's city will be confounded

1 *To the choirmaster. Accor• ing to "Mahalath." Maskil. Of Davi•.*

* The fool hath said in his heart,
"There is no God."
* 2 They are corrupt and do abominable deeds;
there is none that doeth good.

* 3 God looked down from heaven
on the children of men
* to see if there was any that had insight,
that sought after God.

* 4 All have turned away;
they are all alike corrupt.
* There is none that doeth good,
not even one.

* 5 Shall not all the wrongdoers know, †
who eat up My people as they eat bread?
They do not call upon God.

* 6 There they were in great dread,
with nothing to dread.
* Because God hath scattered the bones of thy besiegers; †
they have been put to shame,
because God hath rejected them.

* 7 Who shall give the salvation of Israel out of Zion? †
When God restoreth the fortunes of His people,
Jacob shall exult and Israel be glad.

Psalm 54 (53)

Deus, in nomine tuo

The arrogant set not God before them

1 *To the choirmaster: with strings. Maskil of Davi•,*
2 *when the Ziphites went an• sai• to Saul, "Is not Davi• hi•ing among us?"*

* 3 O God, save me by Thy name,
and judge me by Thy might.
* 4 O God, hear my prayer;
give ear to the words of my mouth.

* 5 For arrogant men have risen up against me, †
and overbearing men have sought after my soul.
They have not set God before them. *Selah*

* 6 Behold, God is my helper;
the Lord is the upholder of my life.
* 7 Turn back the evil upon my adversaries;
in Thy truth, destroy them.

* 8 Willingly will I sacrifice to Thee;
I will give thanks to Thy name, O LORD, for it is good.
* 9 For He hath delivered me out of all trouble,
and my eye hath gazed upon my enemies.

Psalm 55 (54)

Exau•i, Deus

"Cast all your care upon Him, because He cares for you"
(1 Peter 5:7)

1 *To the choirmaster: with strings. Maskil of Davi•.*

* 2 Give ear to my prayer, O God,
and hide not Thyself from my supplication;
* 3 attend to me and answer me.
I am subdued in my meditation and distraught
* 4 at the voice of the enemy,
because of the oppression of the wicked.
* For they bring down wrong upon me,
and in anger they are hostile to me.

* 5 My heart writheth within me,
and the terrors of death have fallen upon me.
* 6 Fear and trembling have come upon me,
and horror hath covered me.

* 7 And I said, "O that I had wings like a dove,
and I would fly away and be at rest.
* 8 Lo, I would wander afar
and lodge in the wilderness. *Selah*
* 9 I would hasten to my place of escape
from the raging wind and tempest."

* 10 Confuse, O Lord, divide their tongues, †
for I have seen violence and strife in the city.
11 Day and night they go around it on its walls.
* 12 Both wrong and trouble are in the midst of it;
ruin is in its midst,
* and oppression and deceit depart not
from its public places.

* 13 For if an enemy had taunted me,
then I could have borne it.

* If one who hated me had magnified himself against me,
then I could have hidden myself from him.
* 14 But it is thou, a man of my rank,
my familiar and my friend.
* 15 We used to take sweet counsel together;
in the house of God, we would walk in the throng.

* 16 Let death come upon them;
let them go down alive into hell;
* for evils are in their habitations,
in their very midst.

* 17 But I will call upon God,
and the LORD will save me.
* 18 Evening, and morning, and at noon, †
I will meditate and moan,
and He will hear my voice.

* 19 He will redeem my soul in peace †
from the battle against me,
for there are many that oppose me.

* 20 God will hear and will humble them,
He Who abideth from of old. *Selah*
* For there is no change with them,
and they fear not God.

* 21 He stretched forth his hand against those at peace with him;
he profaned his covenant.
* 22 His mouth was smoother than butter,
but war was in his heart;
* his words were softer than oil,
but they were drawn swords.

* 23 Cast thy care upon the LORD,
and He will sustain thee;
* He will never allow
the just to be moved.

* 24 But Thou, O God, wilt bring them down
into the pit of destruction.
* Men of blood and deceit †
shall not live out half their days.
But I will trust in Thee.

Psalm 56 (55)

Miserere mei, Deus

"Thy vows are upon me, O God"

1 *To the choirmaster. According to "The silent dove of the faraway places." A miktam of David. When the Philistines seized him in Gath.*

* 2 Be gracious to me, O God, †
for man hath trampled upon me;
fighting all day long, he oppresseth me.
* 3 My adversaries have trampled upon me all day long,
for many fight against me, O Most High.

* 4 On the day when I shall fear,
I will trust in Thee.
* 5 In God — I will praise His word — †
in God I trust; I shall not fear.
What can flesh do to me?

* 6 All day long they disturb my affairs;
all their designs are against me for evil.
* 7 They band together, they lurk,
they observe my steps.
* As they have waited for my soul, †
8 so requite them for their wrong;
in anger cast down the peoples, O God.

* 9 Thou hast counted up my wanderings; †
put my tears into Thy bottle of skin.
Are they not in Thy book?

* 10 Then shall my enemies be turned back
in the day that I shall call.

* This I know, that God is for me. †
11 In God — I will praise His word —
in the LORD — I will praise His word —
* 12 In God I trust, I shall not fear.
What can man do to me?

* 13 Thy vows are upon me, O God;
I will render thank-offerings to Thee.
* 14 For Thou hast delivered my soul from death,
and my feet from stumbling,
* that I may walk before God
in the light of the living.

Psalm 57 (56)

Miserere mei, Deus

"Thou hast wrought all our works for us" (Isaiah 26:12; cf. v.3b)

1 *To the choirmaster. According to "Do not destroy."*
A miktam of David. When he fled from Saul, in the cave.

* 2 Be gracious to me, O God, be gracious to me,
for in Thee hath my soul taken refuge,
* and in the shadow of Thy wings will I take refuge,
until ruin be overpast.

* 3 I will cry to God Most High,
to God Who will accomplish it for me.
* 4 He will send from heaven and save me; †
He will reproach those that trample upon me. *Selah*
God will send His mercy and His truth.

* [5] My soul lieth down amidst lions
that would devour the sons of men.
* Their teeth are spears and arrows,
and their tongue a sharp sword.

* [6] Be exalted above the heavens, O God;
over all the earth be Thy glory.

* [7] They set a net for my steps;
my soul was bowed down.
* They dug a pit before my face,
and have fallen into it themselves. *Selah*

* [8] My heart is steadfast, O God, †
my heart is steadfast;
[9] I will sing and chant a psalm.
* Awake, O my glory; †
awake, psaltery and harp:
I will awake the dawn.

* [10] I will confess to Thee, O LORD, among the peoples;
I will sing a psalm to Thee among the nations,
* [11] because Thy mercy is great unto the heavens,
and Thy truth unto the clouds.

* [12] Be exalted above the heavens, O God;
over all the earth be Thy glory.

Psalm 58 (57)

Si vere utique

"The just shall be cleansed by seeing the punishment"
(St. Augustine, on v. 11)

1 *To the choirmaster. Accor•ing to "Do not •estroy." A miktam of Davi•.*

* 2 Do you indeed speak justice, ye gods?
Do you judge with equity the sons of men?
* 3 Rather, in your heart you work injustice;
your hands clear the way for violence in the land.

* 4 The wicked have been estranged from the womb;
they have gone astray from birth, speaking lies.
* 5 They have venom like the venom of a serpent;
they are like the deaf asp that stoppeth its ears,
* 6 which will not hear the voice of the charmers,
of the wise caster of spells.

* 7 O God, smash their teeth in their mouth;
shatter the jaw teeth of the lions, O LORD.
* 8 Let them melt away like water that runneth off;
let them wither like grass that is trodden down.
* 9 Let them be like a snail that goeth away melting,
like a woman's untimely birth that hath not seen the sun.

* 10 Before your pots can feel the heat from the thorns,
as one living and glowing with anger, He will sweep them away.
* 11 The just will rejoice when he seeth the vengeance;
he will wash his feet in the blood of the wicked.
* 12 And men will say, "Truly there is fruit for the just.
Truly there is a God judging on earth."

Psalm 59 (58)

Eripe me

"Slay them not [outright], lest my people forget"

1 *To the choirmaster. According to "Do not destroy." A miktam of David.*
When Saul sent men, who watched his house, that they might kill him.

* 2 Deliver me from my enemies, O my God;
from those that rise up against me, set me on high.
* 3 Deliver me from wrongdoers,
and from men of blood save me.

* 4 For lo, they have lain in wait for my soul;
the strong have banded together against me.
* 5 Not for my transgression, nor for my sin, O LORD,
without iniquity of mine, they run and make ready.

* Rouse Thyself to meet me, and see.
6 And Thou, O LORD God of hosts, God of Israel,
* awake to visit all the Gentiles.
Be not gracious to any that faithlessly do wrong. *Selah*

* 7 They return at evening; they bark like dogs
and rove about the city.
* 8 Behold, they belch forth from their mouth; †
swords are on their lips.
"For who doth hear?"
* 9 But Thou, O LORD, shalt laugh at them;
Thou shalt mock at all the Gentiles.

* 10 O my Strength, I will watch for Thee,
for God is my high place.

* 11 The God of my mercy will go before me.
God will let me gaze upon my adversaries.

* [12] Slay them not, lest my people forget. †
Disperse them by Thy power,
and bring them down, O Lord, our shield.

* [13] For the sin of their mouth, the word of their lips,
let them be taken in their pride.
* Because of the cursing and lying that they utter, †
[14] consume them in wrath;
consume them, and they shall be no more,
* that men may know that God ruleth
over Jacob to the ends of the earth. *Selah*

* [15] They return at evening; they bark like dogs
and rove about the city.
* [16] They wander about for food;
they murmur if they do not get their fill.

* [17] But I will sing of Thy strength,
and cry aloud of Thy mercy in the morning,
* for Thou hast been a high place for me,
and a refuge in the day of my distress.

* [18] O my Strength, I will sing a psalm to Thee, †
for God is my high place,
the God of my mercy.

Psalm 60 (59)

Deus, repulisti nos

Prayer for restoration after defeat

1 *To the choirmaster. Accor•ing to "The Lily of Testimony."*
A miktam of Davi•. For instruction.

2 *When he strove with Aram-Naharaim an• Aram-Zoba, an•*
when Joab on his return smote E•om in the Valley of Salt: twelve
thousan• men.

* 3 O God, Thou hast cast us off, breached us.
Thou hast been angry; turn back to us.

* 4 Thou hast made the land quake, Thou hast split it open;
heal its fissures, for it is tottering.
* 5 Thou hast shewn Thy people hard things;
Thou hast made us drink the wine of staggering.

* 6 Thou hast given to those that fear Thee a banner,
to rally to it from the face of the bow. *Selah*
* 7 That Thy beloved may be delivered,
save with Thy right hand and answer us.

* 8 God hath spoken in His sanctuary: †
"I will exult, I will divide up Shechem,
and mete out the valley of Succoth.
* 9 Gilead is Mine, and Manasseh is Mine, †
and Ephraim is the protection of My head;
Judah is My scepter.
* 10 Moab is My washbasin; †
upon Edom I will cast My shoe;
over Philistia I will shout for joy."

* 11 Who will bring me into the fortified city?
Who will lead me to Edom?
* 12 Hast not Thou, O God, cast us off?
And Thou goest not forth, O God, with our armies.

* O give us help from trouble,
for vain is the salvation of man.
* 13 In God we shall do valiantly,
and He will tread down our adversaries.

Psalm 61 (60)

Exaudi, Deus

"The one Church of Christ... cries out from the ends of the earth"
(St. Augustine)

1 *To the choirmaster: with strings. Of David.*

* 2 Hear, O God, my outcry;
attend to my prayer.
* 3 From the end of the earth will I call to Thee,
when my heart is faint.

* Lead me onto a rock
that is higher than I.
* 4 For Thou hast been a refuge for me,
a tower of strength from the face of the enemy.

* 5 Let me sojourn in Thy tabernacle forever;
let me take refuge in the covert of Thy wings. *Selah*
* 6 For Thou, O God, hast heard my vows;
Thou hast given me the heritage of those that fear Thy name.

* 7 Add yet more days to the days of the king;
make his years last from generation to generation.
* 8 May he sit forever in the sight of God;
appoint mercy and truth to preserve him.

* 9 So will I sing psalms to Thy name forever,
as I pay my vows day after day.

Psalm 62 (61)

Nonne Deo

"God alone"

1 *To the choirmaster. According to Jeduthun. A Psalm of David.*

* 2 Unto God alone is my soul still;
from Him is my salvation.
* 3 He alone is my rock and my salvation,
my high place; I shall not be greatly moved.

* 4 How long will you assail a man
to murder him, all of you,
* like a leaning wall,
a pushed-in fence?

* 5 They take counsel only to expel him from his eminence;
they take pleasure in falsehood.
* With their mouth they bless,
but inwardly they curse. *Selah*

* 6 Unto God alone be thou still, O my soul,
for from Him is my expectation.
* 7 He alone is my rock and my salvation,
my high place; I shall not be moved.

* 8 Upon God is my salvation and my glory, †
the rock of my strength;
my refuge is in God.
* 9 Trust in Him at all times, O people. †
Pour out your hearts before Him;
God is a refuge for us. *Selah*

* 10 Common men are only vanity;
noblemen are a falsehood.
* In the balances, they go up;
they amount to vanity together.

* 11 Trust not in oppression,
nor become vain by robbery;
* if wealth bear fruit,
set not your heart upon it.

* 12 God hath spoken once;
these two things have I heard:
* that strength belongeth to God,
13 and that to Thee, O Lord, belongeth mercy.
* For Thou wilt render to each man
according to his works.

Psalm 63 (62)

Deus, Deus meus, a• te

Seeking God at daybreak and in the night watches

1 *A Psalm of Davi•, when he was in the wil•erness of Ju•ah.*

* 2 O God, Thou art my God; †
I seek Thee at dawn;
my soul hath thirsted for Thee.
* My flesh hath longed for Thee,
in a parched and weary land where no water is.
* 3 So have I beheld Thee in the sanctuary,
to see Thy strength and Thy glory.

* 4 Because Thy mercy is better than life,
my lips shall commend Thee.
* 5 So will I bless Thee as long as I live;
in Thy name I will lift up my hands.
* 6 As with marrow and fatness shall my soul be satisfied,
and my mouth shall praise Thee with joyous cries
upon my lips.

* 7 When I remember Thee upon my bed,
I meditate on Thee in the watches of the night,

* 8 for Thou hast been my help,
and in the shadow of Thy wings I shout for joy.
* 9 My soul cleaveth fast to Thee;
Thy right hand upholdeth me.

* 10 But those that seek my soul, to destroy it,
shall go down into the depths of the earth;
* 11 they shall be delivered over to the power of the sword;
they shall be a portion for the foxes.
* 12 But the king shall rejoice in God; †
all that swear by Him shall boast,
because the mouth of those that speak falsehood
shall be stopped.

Psalm 64 (63)

Exau• i, Deus, orationem

"The inward part and heart of a man are deep": for good or for evil

1 *To the choirmaster. A Psalm of Davi•.*

* 2 Hear my voice, O God, in my complaint;
preserve my life from dread of the enemy.
* 3 Hide me from the secret counsel of evildoers,
from the tumult of wrongdoers:

* 4 Who have whetted their tongues like a sword,
who have aimed bitter words as their arrows,
* 5 to shoot from secret places at the blameless;
they shoot at him suddenly and do not fear.

* 6 They are resolute in an evil matter; †
they discuss hiding snares.
They say, "Who will see them?"
* 7 They search out iniquities; †
they have accomplished a thorough search,
for the inward part and heart of a man are deep.

* 8 But God hath shot at them an arrow;
suddenly have they been wounded.
* 9 So their own tongue hath made them stumble,
and all who have seen them have wagged their heads.

* 10 Then did all men fear, †
and declare the works of God,
and get insight into His deeds.

* 11 The just shall rejoice in the LORD, †
and take refuge in Him,
and all the upright of heart shall boast.

Psalm 65 (64)

Te decet hymnus

“Stillness is praise”

1 *To the choirmaster. A Psalm of David. A Song.*

* 2 To Thee stillness is praise,
O God, in Zion;
* and to Thee shall vows be paid,
3 O Thou Who hearest prayer.
* To Thee shall all flesh come
on account of iniquity.
* 4 Though our transgressions may prevail against us,
Thou wilt make atonement for them.

* 5 Blessed is he whom Thou dost choose and bring near,
that he may dwell in Thy courts.
* We shall be satisfied with the goodness of Thy house,
with the holiness of Thy temple.

* 6 With dread deeds of justice
Thou wilt answer us, O God of our salvation,
* the confidence of all the ends of the earth,
and of the distant seas.

* [7] Who establisheth the mountains by Thy power,
being girded with might;
* [8] Who quietest the roaring of the seas, †
the roaring of their waves,
and the tumult of the peoples.

* [9] And so the inhabitants of the ends of the earth
are afraid at Thy signs.
* Thou makest the outgoings of morning and evening
to cry aloud for joy.

* [10] Thou hast visited the earth and watered it, †
greatly enriching it;
the river of God is full of water.

* Thou preparest their grain,
for thus dost Thou prepare it:
* [11] drenching its furrows,
leveling its ridges,
* softening it with showers,
blessing its growth.

* [12] Thou hast crowned the year with Thy goodness, †
and Thy chariot ruts drip with fatness;
[13] the pastures of the wilderness drip.

* And so the hills gird themselves with exultation,
[14] the meadows clothe themselves with sheep,
* and the valleys wrap themselves with grain:
They shout for joy; they even sing.

Psalm 66 (65)

Jubilate Deo

Through fire and water into plenty

[1] *To the choirmaster. A Song. A Psalm.*

* Make jubilation to God, all the earth;
[2] sing a psalm to the glory of His name.
* Make His praise glorious;
[3] say to God, "How terrible are Thy deeds."

* Because of the multitude of Thy strength,
Thy enemies will feign homage to Thee.
* [4] Let all the earth adore Thee and sing a psalm to Thee,
let it sing a psalm to Thy name. *Selah*

* [5] Come and see the works of God,
terrible in His deeds for the sons of men.
* [6] He turned the sea into dry land;
they could pass through the river on foot.

* There did we rejoice in Him,
[7] Who ruleth by His might forever.
* His eyes watch over the nations;
let not the stubborn exalt themselves. *Selah*

* [8] Bless our God, ye peoples,
and make the voice of His praise to be heard,
* [9] Who hath set our soul in life,
and not let our foot be moved.

* [10] For Thou, O God, hast tried us;
Thou hast refined us as silver is refined.
* [11] Thou didst bring us into the snare;
Thou didst lay tribulation on our loins.
* [12] Thou didst let men ride over our heads; †
we went through fire and through water;
but Thou didst bring us out into abundance.

* 13 I will go into Thy house with burnt offerings;
I will pay to Thee my vows,
* 14 for which my lips opened
and my mouth spoke when I was in distress.
* 15 I will offer to Thee burnt offerings of fatlings, †
with the incense of rams;
I will offer to Thee bullocks with goats. *Selah*

* 16 Come and hear, all ye that fear God,
and I will tell what He hath done for my soul.
* 17 I cried to Him with my mouth,
and exaltation was under my tongue.
* 18 If I had regarded wrong in my heart,
the Lord would not have heard.
* 19 But truly God hath heard;
He hath attended to the voice of my prayer.

* 20 Blessed be God, Who hath not turned away my prayer,
nor His mercy from me.

Psalm 67 (66)

Deus misereatur

For the evangelization of peoples

1 *To the choirmaster. With strings. A Psalm. A Song.*

* 2 May God be gracious to us and bless us;
may He make His face to shine upon us, *Selah*
* 3 that Thy way may be known upon earth,
in all nations Thy salvation.

* 4 Let the peoples acclaim Thee, O God;
let all the peoples acclaim Thee.

* 5 Let the nations rejoice and cry aloud, †
for Thou judgest the peoples with equity
and leadest the nations on earth. *Selah*

* [6] Let the peoples acclaim Thee, O God;
let all the peoples acclaim Thee.

* [7] The earth hath given her yield;
may God, our God, bless us.
* [8] May God bless us,
and may all the ends of the earth fear Him.

Psalm 68 (67)

Exurgat Deus

The pilgrim people of God

(cf. Numbers 10:35 and Catechism of the Catholic Church 769)

[1] *To the choirmaster. A Psalm of Davi•. A Song.*

* [2] Let God arise, let His enemies be scattered,
and let those that hate Him flee before His face.
* [3] As smoke is driven away, so drive them away; †
as wax melteth at the presence of fire,
so let the wicked perish at the presence of God.

* [4] But let the just rejoice and exult before God,
and let them be jubilant with joy.
* [5] Sing to God, chant a psalm to His name;
cast up a highway for Him Who rideth on the clouds.
* LORD is His name:
Exult ye before Him.

* [6] The father of the fatherless and the judge of widows
is God in His holy habitation.
* [7] God settleth the solitary in a house; †
He bringeth forth the prisoners into prosperity,
but the stubborn dwell in a parched land.

* [8] O God, when Thou wentest forth before Thy people,
when Thou didst march through the wilderness, *Selah*

* [9] the earth quaked, and the heavens also dripped, †
at the presence of God, the One of Sinai,
at the presence of the God of Israel.

* [10] A generous rain Thou didst shed abroad, O God;
when Thy inheritance grew weary, Thou didst restore it.
* [11] Thy community dwelt in it; †
in Thy goodness, O God,
Thou didst provide for the poor.

* [12] The Lord giveth the word;
the women that tell the good tidings are a great host.
* [13] "The kings of the armies, they flee, they flee!" †
And the fair women at home divide the spoils,
[14] although you lie idle among the sheepfolds.
* The wings of a dove are covered with silver,
and her pinions with green gold.
* [15] When the Almighty scattered the kings over it,
snow fell on Zalmon.

* [16] A mountain of God is the mountain of Bashan;
a mountain of peaks is the mountain of Bashan.
* [17] Why eye with envy, O mountain of peaks, †
the mountain that God desired for His dwelling?
Indeed, the LORD will abide there forever.

* [18] The chariots of God are a double myriad, †
thousands upon thousands.
The Lord came from Sinai into the sanctuary.
* [19] Thou hast ascended on high,
Thou hast led captivity captive,
* Thou hast received gifts among men,
even the stubborn, that the LORD God, might dwell there.

* [20] Blessed be the Lord day by day;
He beareth us up, the God of our salvation. *Selah*
* [21] Our God is the God of salvation,
and to the LORD, my Lord, belongeth escape from death.

* [22] But God will smite the heads of His enemies,
the hairy crown of him who walketh about in his guilt.

* [23] The Lord said, "I will bring them back from Bashan,
I will bring them back from the depths of the sea,
* [24] that thy foot may be dipped in blood,
that the tongues of thy dogs may have their portion
from the enemies."

* [25] They have seen Thy processions, O God,
the processions of my God, my king, into the sanctuary:
* [26] The singers in front, the minstrels last,
in the midst of virgins sounding timbrels.

* [27] In the assemblies bless ye God,
the LORD, O ye from the fountain of Israel.
* [28] There is little Benjamin leading them, †
the princes of Judah with their throng,
the princes of Zebulun, the princes of Naphtali.

* [29] Command Thy strength, O God,
the strength by which, O God, Thou hast worked for us.
* [30] Because of Thy temple above Jerusalem,
kings shall bring presents to Thee.

* [31] Rebuke the wild beast of the reeds,
the congregation of bulls with the calves of the peoples.
* Let them prostrate themselves with bars of silver.
Scatter the peoples that want war.
* [32] Nobles shall come from Egypt;
Ethiopia shall hasten to stretch forth her hands to God.

* [33] Sing to God, ye kingdoms of the earth; †
chant a psalm to the Lord, *Selah*
[34] to Him Who rideth upon the heaven of heavens in the east.
* Lo, He uttereth His voice, the voice of strength.
[35] Ascribe ye strength to God.

*   His majesty is over Israel, †
and His strength is in the clouds.
36 Terrible is God from His sanctuary.

*   He is the God of Israel. †
He giveth strength and vigour to His people:
Blessed be God.

Psalm 69 (68)

Salvum me fac, Deus

Good zeal rewarded with gall and vinegar
(cf. John 2:17; Matthew 27:34, 48)

1 *To the choirmaster. According to Lilies. Of David.*

* 2 Save me, O God,
for the waters have come in even unto my soul.

* 3 I have sunk into the mire of the deep,
and there is no standing.
*   I have come into the watery depths,
and the flood hath overwhelmed me.

* 4 I am weary with my calling out;
my throat is hoarse.
*   My eyes have failed
from hoping for my God.

* 5 More numerous than the hairs of my head
are those that hate me without cause.
*   Those that would destroy me are mighty,
my lying enemies.
*   What I took not away,
I must now restore.
* 6 O God, Thou knowest my folly,
and my guilt is not hidden from Thee.

* [7] Let not those who wait for Thee be ashamed
through me,
O Lord, LORD of hosts.
* Let not those who seek Thee be disgraced through me,
O God of Israel.

* [8] Because for Thy sake I have borne reproach;
disgrace hath covered my face.
* [9] I have become a stranger to my brethren,
and an alien to my mother's sons,
* [10] because the zeal of Thy house hath eaten me up,
and the reproaches of them that reproach Thee are
fallen upon me.

* [11] When my soul wept in fasting,
then it became a reproach to me.
* [12] When I made sackcloth my clothing,
then I became a byword to them.
* [13] Those that sit at the gate talk about me,
and the songs of the drunkards are about me.

* [14] But as for me, my prayer is to Thee, O LORD.
At the time of Thy good pleasure, O God,
* in the multitude of Thy mercy, answer me
with the truth of Thy salvation.

* [15] Deliver me out of the mire, that I may not sink; †
let me be delivered from those that hate me,
and from the watery depths.
* [16] Let not the flood waters overwhelm me, †
nor the deep swallow me up,
nor the pit shut its mouth over me.

* [17] Answer me, O LORD, for Thy mercy is good;
according to the multitude of Thy compassions,
turn to me.
* [18] And turn not away Thy face from Thy servant,
for I am in distress — make haste to answer me.

* [19] Draw near to my soul, redeem it;
ransom me because of my enemies.

* [20] Thou knowest my reproach,
and my shame and my disgrace.
* All my adversaries are before Thee;
[21] reproach hath broken my heart, and I am incurable.
* And I expected sympathy, but there was none,
and comforters, but I found none.
* [22] Rather they gave me gall for my food,
and in my thirst, they gave me vinegar to drink.

* [23] Let their table before them become a snare
and a retribution and a stumbling block.
* [24] Let their eyes be darkened, so that they see not,
and make their loins shake continually.
* [25] Pour out Thy indignation upon them,
and let Thy burning anger overtake them.
* [26] Let their encampment be desolate,
with no one dwelling in their tents.
* [27] Because they persecute him whom Thou hast smitten;
they add to the pain of him whom Thou hast wounded.

* [28] Put to their charge iniquity upon iniquity,
and let them not come into Thy justice.
* [29] Let them be blotted out of the book of life
and not be written with the just.

* [30] But I am poor and in pain;
let Thy salvation, O God, set me on high.

* [31] I will praise the name of God with a song,
and I will magnify Him with thanksgiving.
* [32] And it shall please the LORD more than an ox,
more than a bullock, horned and hoofed.

* [33] The humble will see and rejoice;
ye that seek God, your heart shall live.
* [34] For the LORD heareth the needy,
and despiseth not His prisoners.

* 35 Let the heavens and the earth praise Him,
the seas, and all that moveth therein.

* 36 For God will save Zion
and build up the cities of Judah.
* And they shall abide there and possess it. †
37 And the seed of His servants shall inherit it,
and they that love His name shall dwell therein.

Psalm 70 (69)

Deus, in adiutorium meum intende

"O God, to deliver me – O Lord, to my help, make haste"

(cf. v.2, Hebrew)

1 *To the choirmaster. A Psalm of David. For a commemoration.*

* 2 Incline unto my aid, O God;
O LORD, make haste to help me.

* 3 Let them be ashamed and confounded
that seek my soul.
* Let them be turned back and disgraced
that wish me evil.
* 4 Let them turn back because of their shame
that say, "Aha, aha."

* 5 May all that seek Thee
rejoice and be glad in Thee.
* And may such as love Thy salvation
say continually, "Let God be magnified."

* 6 But I am poor and needy;
O God, hasten to me.
* Thou art my help and my deliverer;
O LORD, make no delay.

Psalm 71 (70)

In te, Domine, speravi

"Upon Thee have I leaned from [within] the womb"

* 1 In Thee, O LORD, have I taken refuge;
Let me never be ashamed.
* 2 In Thy justice deliver me and rescue me;
incline Thy ear unto me and save me.

* 3 Be Thou to me a rock of refuge
to which I may always go.
* Thou hast commanded my salvation,
for Thou art my rock and my fortress.
* 4 O my God, rescue me from the hand of the wicked,
and from the grasp of the unjust and the oppressor.

* 5 For Thou art my expectation, O Lord,
my trust, O LORD, from my youth.
* 6 Upon Thee have I leaned from the womb; †
Thou art He Who took me from within my mother;
my praise is continually of Thee.

* 7 I have been as a portent to many,
but Thou art my strong refuge.
* 8 My mouth shall be filled with Thy praise,
with Thy beauty all the day.

* 9 Cast me not off in the time of old age;
when my strength shall fail, do not Thou forsake me.

* 10 For my enemies have talked about me,
and those that watch my soul have consulted together,
* 11 saying, "God hath forsaken him.
Pursue and seize him, for there is none to deliver him."
* 12 O God, be not far from me;
O my God, make haste to help me.

* 13 Let them be ashamed and come to an end,
that are the accusers of my soul;

* let them be covered with reproach and disgrace,
that seek my evil.

* [14] But I will always hope,
and will add to all Thy praise.
* [15] My mouth shall tell of Thy justice, †
every day of Thy salvation,
although I know not their number.

* [16] I will come with the mighty deeds of the Lord;
I will commemorate, O LORD, Thy justice, Thine alone.
* [17] O God, Thou hast taught me from my youth,
and until now I declare Thy wonders.

* [18] And even unto old age and gray hairs,
O God, forsake me not,
* until I declare Thy arm
to the generation that is to come.
* [19] Thy might and Thy justice, O God,
reach to the heights.
* Thou Who hast done great things —
O God, who is like Thee?

* [20] Thou Who hast made me see many and sore troubles
wilt quicken me again,
* and from the depths of the earth
Thou wilt bring me up again.
* [21] Thou wilt multiply my greatness,
and turn and comfort me.

* [22] So I will give thanks to Thee upon the psaltery
for Thy truth, O my God.
* I will sing a psalm to Thee upon the harp,
O Holy One of Israel.
* [23] My lips shall cry aloud, †
when I sing a psalm to Thee,
and my soul also, which Thou hast redeemed.

* [24] And so my tongue shall meditate
on Thy justice all the day,
* for they are shamed and confounded
that sought to do me evil.

Psalm 72 (71)

Deus, judicium tuum

"The work of justice shall be peace" (Isaiah 32:17)

1 *A Psalm of Solomon.*

* O God, give Thy judgment to the king,
and Thy justice to the son of a king.
* 2 May he judge Thy people with justice,
and Thy poor with judgment.

* 3 Let the mountains bring peace for the people,
and the hills justice.
* 4 He shall judge the poor of the people, †
save the children of the needy,
and crush the oppressor.

* 5 And he will prolong his days with the sun
and before the moon,
throughout all generations.
* 6 He shall descend like rain upon the mown grass,
like showers that richly moisten the earth.

* 7 In his days justice shall flourish,
and abundance of peace, till the moon be no more.
* 8 And he shall have dominion from sea to sea,
and from the river to the ends of the earth.

* 9 Before him the desert dwellers shall fall down,
and his enemies lick the dust.
* 10 The kings of Tarshish and the islands
shall offer presents.
* The kings of Sheba and Seba
shall bring gifts.
* 11 And all kings shall adore him;
all nations shall serve him.

* 12 For he shall deliver the needy who crieth out,
and the poor who hath no helper.
* 13 He shall have pity on the weak and the needy,
and the souls of the needy he shall save.
* 14 From usuries and violence he shall redeem their souls,
and their blood shall be precious in his sight.

* 15 So may he live,
and the gold of Sheba be given to him;
* and they shall pray for him continually;
all the day shall they bless him.

* 16 There shall be an abundance of grain in the land; †
on the mountaintops shall it wave;
its fruit shall be like Lebanon;
* and they shall blossom forth from the city
like the grass of the land.

* 17 May his name be everlasting;
before the sun shall his name continue.
* And men shall be blessed in him,
all nations call him blessed.

* 18 Blessed be the LORD God, the God of Israel,
Who alone doth wonderful things.
* 19 And blessed be His glorious name forever; †
and may the whole earth be filled with His glory.
Amen and amen.

20 *The prayers of David, the son of Jesse, are ended.*

BOOK III

Psalms 73-89

(The •ecline of Davi•'s king•om)

Psalm 73 (72)

Quam bonus Israel Deus

The last things of the proud and of the pure of heart

1 *A Psalm of Asaph.*

* Surely God is good to Israel,
to the pure of heart.
* 2 But as for me, my feet had almost stumbled,
my steps had well-nigh slipped,
* 3 for I was envious of the boastful,
when I saw the peace of the wicked.

* 4 For there are no pangs for them;
their bodies are sound and fat.
* 5 They need not toil like men,
nor are they stricken like other men.
* 6 Therefore pride is their necklace;
violence covereth them like a garment.
* 7 Their eyes bulge through fatness;
their hearts overflow with conceits.

* 8 They scoff and speak with malice;
from on high they speak oppression.

* 9 They have set their mouth against heaven,
and their tongue goeth through the earth.
* 10 Therefore the people turn to them,
and drink up the water of their words.
* 11 And they say, "How doth God know,
and is there knowledge in the Most High?"
* 12 Behold, these are the wicked,
and ever at ease, they make great their wealth.

* 13 Surely in vain have I kept my heart clean,
and washed my hands in innocence,
* 14 for I have been stricken all day long,
and rebuked every morning.
* 15 If I had said, "I will speak thus,"
behold, I would have betrayed the generation
of Thy children.

* 16 When I considered how I might know this thing,
it was laborious in my sight,
* 17 until I entered into the sanctuary of God,
and understood their latter end:

* 18 Surely Thou wilt set them in slippery places;
Thou makest them fall into ruin.
* 19 How they come to desolation in a moment,
swept away, finished by terrors!
* 20 As a dream at awaking, O Lord,
when Thou rousest Thyself, Thou shalt despise
their shadow.

* 21 When my heart was embittered,
and my reins were pierced,
* 22 then I was reduced to naught, and I knew it not;
I was like a beast with Thee.

* 23 Yet I am continually with Thee;
Thou hast taken hold of my right hand.
* 24 Thou wilt lead me by Thy counsel,
and hereafter receive me to glory.

* 25 Whom have I in heaven?
And having Thee, I want nothing on earth.
* 26 Though my flesh and my heart may fail,
God is the rock of my heart and my portion forever.

* 27 For lo, they that are far from Thee shall perish;
Thou destroyest every fornicator from Thy presence.
* 28 But for me, the nearness of God is my good; †
I have made the Lord God my refuge,
that I may recount all Thy works.

Psalm 74 (73)

Ut qui•, Deus

"The Lord hath put to oblivion appointed feast and sabbath"
(Lamentations 2: 6b)

1 *A Maskil of Asaph.*

* Why, O God, hast Thou cast us off forever?
Why doth Thy anger smoke against the sheep
of Thy pasture?
* 2 Remember Thy congregation, which Thou hast acquired
of old, †
which Thou hast redeemed as the tribe of Thy inheritance,
Mount Zion, in which Thou hast dwelt.

* 3 Lift up Thy steps to the perpetual ruins;
the enemy hath laid waste everything in the sanctuary.
* 4 Thy adversaries have roared in Thy meeting-place;
they have set up their own signs for signs.

* 5 It was like men wielding axes
in the midst of a thicket of trees.
* 6 And then its carved work altogether
they struck down with axes and hatchets.

* 7 They set Thy sanctuary on fire;
they profaned to the ground the dwelling place of Thy name.

* 8 They said in their heart, "Let us altogether oppress them."
They burned all the meeting-places of God in the land.
* 9 We do not see our signs; †
there is no longer any prophet,
nor is there any among us who knoweth how long.

* 10 How long, O God, shall the adversary taunt?
Shall the enemy spurn Thy name forever?
* 11 Why dost Thou draw back Thy hand,
and keep Thy right hand in the midst of Thy bosom?

* 12 Yet God my king is from of old,
working deeds of salvation in the midst of the earth.
* 13 Thou didst split the sea by Thy strength;
Thou didst shatter the heads of the dragons on the waters.
* 14 Thou didst crush the heads of Leviathan;
Thou didst give him for food to the creatures of the desert.
* 15 Thou hast cloven open springs and streams;
Thou hast dried up ever-flowing rivers.

* 16 Thine is the day, Thine also is the night;
Thou hast established the luminaries and the sun.
* 17 Thou hast fixed all the bounds of the earth;
summer and winter — Thou hast formed them.

* 18 Remember this, the enemy hath taunted the LORD,
and a foolish people hath scorned Thy name.
* 19 Deliver not to the wild beasts the soul of Thy turtledove;
the life of Thy poor ones forget not forever.

* 20 Have regard for the covenant, for the dark places of the land
are filled with the habitations of violence.
* 21 Let not the oppressed turn back disgraced;
let the poor and the needy praise Thy name.

* 22 Arise, O God, plead Thy cause;
remember Thy reproach from the fool all the day.
* 23 Forget not the voice of Thy adversaries,
the uproar of Thy opponents that ascendeth continually.

Psalm 75 (74)

Confitebimur tibi

Judgment at the appointed time

1 *To the choirmaster. According to "Do not destroy." A Psalm of Asaph. A Song.*

* 2 We give Thee thanks, O God; †
we give Thee thanks, for near is Thy name;
they recount Thy wonders.

* 3 "When I seize the time,
I Myself will judge with equity.
* 4 Though the earth totter and all that dwell therein,
it is I Who steady its pillars." *Selah*

* 5 I have said to the boastful: "Boast not,"
and to the wicked: "Exalt not your horn.
* 6 Exalt not your horn on high;
speak not with insolent neck."
* 7 For neither from the east, nor from the west,
nor from the wilderness cometh exaltation.
* 8 For God is the judge:
One He putteth down, and another He exalteth.

* 9 For there is a cup in the hand of the LORD,
and the wine is foaming, fully mixed.
* And He will pour from it, and they shall drain even its dregs:
All the wicked of the earth shall drink.

* [10] But I will declare it forever;
I will sing a psalm to the God of Jacob:
* [11] "And all the horns of the wicked I will hack off,
but the horns of the just shall be exalted."

Psalm 76 (75)

Notus in Ju•aea

"The earth feared and was quiet, when God arose for judgment"
(cf. Matthew 28:4)

[1] *To the choirmaster: with strings. A Psalm of Asaph. A Song.*

* [2] In Judah, God is known;
in Israel His name is great.
* [3] And His tabernacle is in Salem,
and His dwelling place in Zion.
* [4] There He broke the flashing shafts of the bow,
the shield, the sword, and the battle. *Selah*

* [5] Resplendent art Thou,
more magnificent than the everlasting mountains.
* [6] The stouthearted were despoiled; †
they slept their sleep,
and none of the men of valour could find their hands.
* [7] At Thy rebuke, O God of Jacob,
both rider and horse fell fast asleep.

* [8] Thou, terrible art Thou,
and who shall withstand Thee at the time of Thy anger?
* [9] From heaven Thou didst make Thy judgment heard;
the earth feared and was quiet,
* [10] when God arose for judgment,
to save all the meek of the earth. *Selah*

* 11 For the wrath of man shall praise Thee,
and the remnant of wrath Thou shalt gird upon Thee.
* 12 Vow and pay to the LORD your God;
let all around Him bring gifts to the One to be feared,
* 13 Who cutteth off the spirit of princes,
Who is terrible to the kings of the earth.

Psalm 77 (76)

Voce mea

"The everlasting years"

1 *To the choirmaster. Accor•ing to Je•uthan. A Psalm of Asaph.*

* 2 With my voice I cried to God —
with my voice to God, that He might give ear to me.

* 3 In the day of my distress I sought the Lord; †
my hand was stretched forth at night and did not grow feeble.
My soul refused to be comforted.
* 4 I remember my God and I groan;
I meditate, and my spirit fainteth. *Selah*

* 5 Thou heldest open my eyelids;
I was troubled and could not speak.
* 6 I considered the days of old;
I remembered the everlasting years.
* 7 I meditated at night with my heart;
I pondered, and my spirit searched.

* 8 Will the Lord cast off forever,
and never again be favourable?
* 9 Hath His mercy ended forever?
Is His word completed for all generations?
* 10 Hath God forgotten to be gracious,
or in anger shut up His compassion? *Selah*

* [11] And I said, "This is what pierceth me:
the change of the right hand of the Most High."

* [12] I will remember the deeds of the LORD,
when I remember Thy wonders from of old.
* [13] And I will meditate on all Thy works,
and reflect on Thy acts.

* [14] O God, Thy way is in holiness;
who is a great god like God?
* [15] Thou art the God Who workest wonders;
Thou hast made known Thy strength among the peoples.
* [16] With Thy arm Thou hast redeemed Thy people,
the children of Jacob and Joseph. *Selah*

* [17] The waters saw Thee, O God, †
the waters saw Thee and writhed;
the very depths trembled.
* [18] The clouds poured out water; †
the skies gave voice;
Thy arrows also went to and fro.
* [19] The voice of Thy thunder was in the whirlwind, †
Thy lightnings lighted up the world;
the earth trembled and quaked.

* [20] Thy way was in the sea, †
and Thy path in the many waters,
but Thy footprints were not known.

* [21] Thou didst lead Thy people like a flock,
by the hand of Moses and Aaron.

Psalm 78 (77)

Atten•ite

Forget not the deeds of God

[1] *A Maskil of Asaph.*

* Give ear, O my people, to my teaching;
incline your ear to the words of my mouth.
* [2] I will open my mouth in a parable;
I will utter dark sayings from of old.

* [3] The things that we have heard and known,
and that our fathers have told us,
* [4] we will not hide from their children,
telling to the generation to come
* the praises of the LORD and His strength,
and His wonders that He did.

* [5] For He established a testimony in Jacob,
and put a law in Israel,
* which He commanded to our fathers,
to make them known to their children,
* [6] that the generation to come might know,
the children yet to be born.

* They should rise up and tell them to their children,
[7] so that they should put their confidence in God,
* and not forget the deeds of God,
but keep His commandments;
* [8] that they might not be like their fathers,
a stubborn and rebellious generation,
* a generation that did not make its heart steadfast,
and whose spirit was not faithful to God.

* [9] The sons of Ephraim, well-armed archers,
turned back in the day of battle.
* [10] They kept not the covenant of God,
and refused to walk in His law.

* [11] And they forgot His deeds,
and His wonders that He had shewn them.
* [12] In the sight of their fathers He did marvels,
in the land of Egypt, in the plain of Zoan.

* [13] He split the sea and brought them through,
and made the waters stand like a wall.
* [14] And He led them with a cloud by day,
and all the night by the light of fire.
* [15] He split rocks in the wilderness,
and gave them drink as from the great deep.
* [16] And He brought forth streams from the rock,
and made waters run down like rivers.

* [17] But they sinned still more against Him,
rebelling against the Most High in the parched land.
* [18] And they tempted God in their hearts
by asking food for their souls.
* [19] And they spoke against God;
they said, "Can God prepare a table in the wilderness?
* [20] Behold, He struck the rock, and the waters gushed out,
and the streams overflowed.
* Can He also give bread,
or provide meat for His people?"

* [21] Therefore the LORD heard and was enraged, †
and a fire was kindled against Jacob,
and anger rose against Israel,
* [22] because they believed not in God,
and trusted not in His salvation.

* [23] But He commanded the clouds from above,
and opened the doors of heaven.
* [24] And He rained upon them manna to eat,
and gave them grain from heaven:
* [25] Man ate the bread of angels;
He sent them provisions in abundance.
* [26] He stirred up the east wind in heaven,
and by His strength He led forth the south wind.

* [27] And He rained upon them flesh as dust,
and wingèd fowl as the sand of the sea,
* [28] and they fell in the midst of their camp,
round about their habitations.
* [29] And they ate and were well sated,
for He had brought them what they craved.

* [30] They had not turned aside from their craving,
their food was still in their mouths,
* [31] when the anger of God rose against them, †
and He slew the fattest among them,
and laid low the chosen of Israel.

* [32] Despite all this they still sinned
and believed not in His wondrous works,
* [33] so He ended their days in vanity,
and their years with dispatch.

* [34] When He slew them, then they would seek Him;
they repented and sought God at dawn.
* [35] And they remembered that God was their rock,
and the Most High God their redeemer.
* [36] But they persuaded Him with their mouth,
and lied to Him with their tongue,
* [37] for their heart was not steadfast with Him,
nor were they faithful to His covenant.

* [38] And He, being compassionate,
maketh atonement for iniquity and destroyeth not.
* Often doth He turn away His anger
and not stir up all His wrath.
* [39] So He remembered that they are flesh,
a wind that goeth by and returneth not.
* [40] How often did they rebel against Him in the wilderness,
grieve Him in the wasteland!

* [41] And they turned back and tempted God,
and provoked the Holy One of Israel.

* 42 They did not remember His hand,
the day that He redeemed them from the adversary,
* 43 when He set His signs in Egypt,
and His portents in the plain of Zoan.

* 44 He turned their rivers into blood,
and their streams, so they could not drink.
* 45 He sent among them swarms of flies, which devoured them,
and frogs, which destroyed them.
* 46 And He gave their produce to the caterpillar,
and their labour to the locust.
* 47 He killed their vines with hail,
and their sycamores with frost.
* 48 He consigned their cattle to hail,
and their flocks to fiery bolts.

* 49 He sent on them the heat of His anger, †
rage, and indignation, and distress,
a mission of angels of evil.
* 50 He cleared a path for His anger; †
He spared not their souls from death,
but consigned their life to the plague.
* 51 He smote all the firstborn in Egypt,
the firstfruits of their vigour in the tents of Ham.

* 52 He took away His people like sheep,
and guided them in the wilderness like a flock.
* 53 He led them securely, and they feared not,
but the sea covered their enemies.
* 54 And He brought them to His holy border,
to this mountain that His right hand acquired.
* 55 And He drove out the nations before them, †
and allotted them by measuring line for an inheritance,
and made the tribes of Israel to dwell in their tents.

* 56 Yet they tempted and rebelled against God Most High,
and they kept not His testimonies.

* 57 So they turned away and were faithless like their fathers;
they twisted like a treacherous bow.
* 58 Thus they provoked Him with their high places,
and aroused His jealousy with their graven images.

* 59 God heard and was enraged,
and He utterly rejected Israel.
* 60 And He abandoned the tabernacle of Shiloh,
the tent where He dwelt among men.
* 61 And He delivered His strength into captivity,
and His beauty into the hand of the adversary.
* 62 And He consigned His people to the sword,
and was enraged at His inheritance.
* 63 Fire devoured their young men,
and their virgins were not praised in wedding songs.
* 64 Their priests fell by the sword,
and their widows were not able to weep.

* 65 Then the Lord awoke as from sleep,
like a mighty man surfeited with wine.
* 66 And He struck His adversaries backwards;
He put them to everlasting reproach.

* 67 And He rejected the tabernacle of Joseph,
and the tribe of Ephraim He chose not,
* 68 but He chose the tribe of Judah,
Mount Zion, which He loved.
* 69 And He built His sanctuary like the heights,
like the earth, which He hath founded forever.

* 70 And He chose David His servant,
and took him from the sheepfolds;
* 71 from following the nursing ewes He brought him †
to shepherd Jacob His people,
and Israel His inheritance.
* 72 So he shepherded them in the integrity of his heart,
and with understanding hands, he led them.

Psalm 79 (78)

Deus, venerunt gentes

"O Jerusalem, He Who named thee will comfort thee"
(Baruch 4: 30)

1 *A Psalm of Asaph.*

* O God, the heathen have come into Thy inheritance; †
they have defiled Thy holy temple;
they have laid Jerusalem in heaps of ruins.
* 2 They have given the corpses of Thy servants †
as food for the birds of heaven,
the flesh of Thy saints to the beasts of the earth.
* 3 They have poured out their blood like water †
round about Jerusalem,
and there was none to bury them.
* 4 We have become a reproach to our neighbours,
a mockery and a derision to those round about us.

* 5 How long, O LORD? Wilt Thou be angry forever?
Will Thy jealousy burn like fire?
* 6 Pour out Thy wrath upon the nations that have not
known Thee,
and upon the kingdoms that have not called
upon Thy name.
* 7 For they have devoured Jacob,
and laid waste his habitation.

* 8 Remember not against us the iniquities of our forefathers; †
let Thy compassion come speedily to meet us,
for we are brought very low.
* 9 Help us, O God of our salvation,
for the glory of Thy name,
* and deliver us and make atonement for our sins,
for Thy name's sake.

* [10] Why should the heathen say, "Where is their God?" †
Let there be known among the heathen before our eyes,
the avenging of the outpoured blood of Thy servants.

* [11] Let the groaning of the prisoners come before Thee;
according to the greatness of Thy arm, preserve those doomed to death.

* [12] And render to our neighbours sevenfold into their bosom
their reproach wherewith they have reproached Thee, O LORD.

* [13] But we, Thy people, and the sheep of Thy pasture, †
will give thanks to Thee forever;
from generation to generation we will tell Thy praise.

Psalm 80 (79)

Qui regis Israel

***Ecclesia semper reformanda*: "The Church, ever to be reformed"**

1 *To the choirmaster. Accor• ing to Lilies. A testimony of Asaph. A Psalm.*

* 2 Give ear, O shepherd of Israel,
Thou that guidest Joseph like a flock.
* Thou that sittest upon the cherubim, shine forth †
3 before Ephraim and Benjamin and Manasseh;
stir up Thy might and come to save us.

* 4 O God, convert us;
let Thy face shine, and we shall be saved.

* 5 O LORD God of hosts, how long
wilt Thou smoke against the prayer of Thy people?
* 6 Thou hast fed them with the bread of tears,
and given them tears to drink in full measure.
* 7 Thou hast put us in contention with our neighbours,
and our enemies mock at us.

* 8 O God of hosts, convert us;
let Thy face shine, and we shall be saved.

* 9 Thou didst bring forth a vine from Egypt;
Thou didst drive out the nations and plant it.
* 10 Thou didst clear a place before it;
it struck root and filled the land.

* 11 The mountains were covered with its shadow,
and the cedars of God with its branches;
* 12 it sent out its boughs unto the sea,
and its shoots unto the river.

* 13 Why hast Thou breached its fences,
so that all who pass along the way pluck it?

* 14 The boar from the forest doth ravage it,
and whatever moveth in the field doth feed on it.

* 15 Turn again, O God of hosts, †
look down from heaven and see,
and visit this vine.

* 16 And establish what Thy right hand hath planted,
and the son of man whom Thou hast made firm for Thyself.

* 17 It is burnt with fire, cut down —
May they perish at the rebuke of Thy countenance.

* 18 Let Thy hand be upon the man of Thy right hand,
upon the son of man whom Thou hast made firm for Thyself.

* 19 And we will not turn away from Thee;
quicken us, and we will call upon Thy name.

* 20 O LORD, God of hosts, convert us;
let Thy face shine, and we shall be saved.

Psalm 81 (80)

Exultate Deo

How to be saved? "By willing it"

(St. Thomas Aquinas)

1 *To the choirmaster. Accor• ing to the "Gittith." A Psalm of Asaph.*

* 2 Ring out a cry to God our strength;
make jubilation to the God of Jacob.
* 3 Raise a psalm and sound the timbrel,
the pleasant harp with the psaltery.
* 4 Blow the horn at the new moon,
at the full moon, on our feast day.

* 5 For it is a statute for Israel,
a judgment of the God of Jacob.
* 6 He made it a testimony in Joseph,
when he went out from the land of Egypt.

* A tongue I knew not, I heard: †
7 "I removed his back from the burden;
his hands withdrew from the basket.
* 8 In distress thou didst call, and I delivered thee; †
I answered thee in the secret place of thunder;
I proved thee at the waters of Meribah. *Selah*

* 9 Hear, O My people, as I testify against thee.
O Israel, if thou wouldst but hearken to Me!

* 10 There shall be no strange god among thee,
nor shalt thou adore a foreign god.
* 11 I am the LORD thy God, †
Who brought thee up out of the land of Egypt.
Open thy mouth wide, and I will fill it.

* 12 But My people heard not My voice,
and Israel was unwilling toward Me.
* 13 So I let them go in the stubbornness of their heart;
they shall walk in their own counsels.

* [14] If only My people would hear Me,
if Israel would but walk in My ways!
* [15] In a moment I would humble their enemies
and turn My hand against their adversaries.

* [16] Those who hate the LORD would feign homage to Him,
and their time would last forever.
* [17] But I would feed him with the fat of wheat,
and with honey from the rock I would satisfy him."

Psalm 82 (81)

Deus stetit

Earthly judges are vicars of God (cf. Romans 13:1)

[1] *A Psalm of Asaph.*

* God hath taken His stand in the divine council;
in the midst of the gods He giveth judgment.

* [2] "How long will you judge unjustly,
and lift up the faces of the wicked? *Selah*
* [3] Give judgment for the weak and the fatherless;
do justice to the humble and the poor.
* [4] Rescue the weak and the needy;
deliver them from the hand of the wicked."

* [5] They neither know nor understand; †
they walk about in darkness;
all the foundations of the earth are moved.

* [6] I said, "You are gods,
and sons of the Most High, all of you."
* [7] Nevertheless, you shall die like men,
and fall like one of the princes.

* [8] Arise, O God, judge the earth,
for Thou shalt inherit all the nations.

Psalm 83 (82)

Deus, quis similis

May the foe be abashed and seek the Lord's name

1 *A Song. A Psalm of Asaph.*

* 2 O God, keep not Thou still;
be not silent or quiet, O God.
* 3 For lo, Thy enemies are in an uproar,
and those that hate Thee have lifted up their head.

* 4 They slyly consult against Thy people,
and take counsel against Thy hidden ones.
* 5 They have said, "Come, let us efface them as a nation,
and let the name of Israel be remembered no more."
* 6 For they have taken counsel with one heart;
against Thee they make a covenant:

* 7 The tents of Edom and the Ishmaelites,
Moab and the Hagrites,
* 8 Gebal and Ammon and Amalek,
Philistia with the inhabitants of Tyre.
* 9 Assyria, too, hath joined with them;
they have become an arm for the children of Lot. *Selah*

* 10 Do to them as Thou didst to Midian and to Sisera,
as to Jabin at the brook Kishon,
* 11 who were done away with at Endor,
who became dung for the ground.
* 12 Make their nobles like Oreb and Zeeb,
like Zeba and Zalmunna all their princes,
* 13 who said, "Let us take possession for ourselves
of the pastures of God."
* 14 O my God, make them like a wheel,
as stubble before the wind.

* 15 As a fire burneth a forest,
and as a flame devoureth the mountains,

* 16 so pursue them with Thy tempest,
and dismay them with Thy gale.
* 17 Fill their faces with dishonour,
that they may seek Thy name, O LORD.

* 18 Let them be ashamed and dismayed forever;
let them be confounded and perish.
* 19 And let them know that Thou alone, Whose name is LORD,
art the Most High over all the earth.

Psalm 84 (83)

Quam •ilecta

***Vale of tears*: a life of tribulation; *Blessed*: beatitude past understanding**
(St. Bruno on vv.7 and 5)

1 *To the choirmaster. Accor•ing to the "Gittith." A Psalm of the Sons of Korah.*

* 2 How lovely are Thy tabernacles,
O LORD of hosts!

* 3 My soul hath longed and even fainted
for the courts of the LORD;
* my heart and my flesh cry out
to the living God.

* 4 Even the sparrow hath found herself a house, †
and the swallow a nest for herself,
where she may lay her young,
* at Thy altars, O LORD of hosts,
my king and my God.

* 5 Blessed are they that dwell in Thy house;
ever shall they praise Thee. *Selah*
* 6 Blessed are the men whose strength is in Thee,
in whose hearts are the highways.

* 7 As they pass through the vale of tears, †
they will make it into a spring;
the early rain, too, will cover it with blessings.
* 8 They will go from strength to strength;
the God of gods will be seen in Zion.

* 9 O LORD God of hosts, hear my prayer;
give ear, O God of Jacob. *Selah*
* 10 Behold our shield, O God,
and look upon the face of Thy anointed.

* 11 For better is one day in Thy courts
than a thousand others.
* I would rather stand at the threshold of
the house of my God
than dwell in the tents of wickedness.

* 12 For the LORD God is a sun and a shield;
the Lord will give grace and glory.
* No good thing will He withhold
from those that walk in integrity.

* 13 O LORD of hosts,
blessed is the man that trusteth in Thee.

Psalm 85 (84)

Bene•ixisti, Domine

Christmas: "Truth is sprung up from the earth..."

(St. Augustine)

1 *To the choirmaster. A Psalm of the sons of Korah.*

* 2 O LORD, Thou wast well pleased with Thy land;
Thou didst restore the fortunes of Jacob.
* 3 Thou didst take away the iniquity of Thy people;
Thou didst cover all their sins. *Selah*
* 4 Thou didst withdraw all Thy wrath;
Thou didst turn from Thy burning anger.

* 5 Convert us, O God of our salvation,
and break off Thy vexation with us.
* 6 Wilt Thou be angry with us forever?
Wilt Thou draw out Thy anger from generation to generation?
* 7 Wilt Thou not turn and revive us,
and Thy people shall rejoice in Thee?
* 8 Shew us, O LORD, Thy mercy,
and grant us Thy salvation.

* 9 I will hear what the LORD God will speak, †
for He will speak peace to His people and to His saints,
and to those who turn to Him their heart.
* 10 Surely His salvation is near to them that fear Him,
that glory may dwell in our land.

* 11 Mercy and truth have met each other;
justice and peace have kissed.
* 12 Truth is sprung up from the earth,
and justice hath looked down from heaven.

* 13 And so the LORD will give what is good,
and our land will give its yield.
* 14 Justice shall walk before Him,
and set His steps in the way.

Psalm 86 (85)

Inclina, Domine

"I will give them one heart and one way" (Jeremiah 32:39; cf. v.11c)

1 *A Prayer of David.*

* Incline Thy ear, O LORD, and answer me,
for I am poor and needy.
* 2 Keep my soul, for I am merciful;
save Thy servant, O my God, that trusteth in Thee.

* 3 Be gracious to me, O Lord,
for I cry to Thee all the day.
* 4 Gladden the soul of Thy servant,
for to Thee, O Lord, do I lift up my soul.

* 5 For Thou, O Lord, art sweet and mild,
and abounding in mercy to all that call upon Thee.
* 6 Give ear, O LORD, to my prayer,
and attend to the voice of my supplication.

* 7 In the day of my trouble I will call upon Thee,
for Thou wilt answer me.
* 8 There is none like Thee among the gods, O Lord,
nor any works like Thine.

* 9 All the nations Thou hast made shall come †
and shall adore before Thee, O Lord,
and shall glorify Thy name.
* 10 For Thou art great and dost wonderful things;
Thou art God alone.

* 11 Teach me, O LORD, Thy way, †
that I may walk in Thy truth;
unite my heart to fear Thy name.

* 12 I will thank Thee, O Lord my God, with all my heart,
and I will glorify Thy name forever;

* [13] for great is Thy mercy toward me,
and Thou hast delivered my soul from nethermost hell.

* [14] O God, arrogant men have risen up against me, †
and a band of overbearing men have sought my soul,
and they have not set Thee before them.

* [15] But Thou, O Lord, art a God compassionate and gracious, slow to anger
* and abounding in mercy and truth;
[16] O turn to me, and be gracious to me.

* Give Thy strength to Thy servant,
and save the son of Thy handmaid.
* [17] Work me a sign of good, †
that those who hate me may see and be ashamed,
because Thou, O LORD, hast helped me and comforted me.

Psalm 87 (86)

Fun• amenta ejus

The Church Catholic

[1] *A Psalm of the Sons of Korah. A Song.*

* His foundation is on the holy mountains. †
[2] The LORD loveth the gates of Zion
more than all the tabernacles of Jacob.
* [3] Glorious things are spoken of thee,
O city of God. *Selah*

* [4] I will be mindful of Rahab and Babylon
among those that know Me.
* Behold Philistia and Tyre with Ethiopia:
"This one was born there."

* 5 And of Zion it shall be said: †
"This man and that were born in her."
And the Most High Himself shall establish her.

* 6 The LORD will record in the writing down of the peoples:
"This one was born there." *Selah*
* 7 And they sing, while they dance:
"All my springs are in thee."

Psalm 88 (87)

Domine, Deus salutis meae

"He descended into hell" (Apostles Creed)

1 *A Song. A Psalm of the Sons of Korah. To the choirmaster.*
Accor• ing to "Mahalath Leannoth." A Maskil of Heman the Ezrahite.

* 2 O LORD, the God of my salvation, †
I have cried out by day
before Thee, and in the night.
* 3 Let my prayer come before Thee;
incline Thy ear to my cry.

* 4 For my soul is sated with evils,
and my life hath drawn near to hell.
* 5 I am reckoned with those that go down into the pit;
I have become as a strong man without strength,
* 6 free among the dead,
like the slain sleeping in the sepulchers,
* whom Thou rememberest no more,
for they are cut off from Thy hand.

* 7 Thou hast put me in the lowest pit,
in the dark places, in the depths.
* 8 Thy wrath hath lain hard upon me,
and with all Thy breakers Thou hast humbled me. *Selah*

* [9] Thou hast put my acquaintances far from me;
Thou hast made me an abomination to them.
* I am shut in, and I cannot get out.
[10] My eyes have languished from affliction.

* I have called to Thee, O LORD, all the day;
I have spread out my hands to Thee.
* [11] Wilt Thou work wonders for the dead,
or will the shades rise up and confess to Thee? *Selah*

* [12] Shall Thy mercy be told in the grave,
and Thy faithfulness in the place of perdition?
* [13] Shall Thy wonders be known in the dark,
and Thy justice in the land of oblivion?

* [14] But I have cried to Thee, O LORD, for help,
and in the morning shall my prayer come before Thee.
* [15] O LORD, why dost Thou cast off my soul,
why hidest Thou Thy face from me?

* [16] I am poor and expiring from my youth;
I have borne Thy terrors, I am perplexed.
* [17] Thy fury hath passed over me,
and Thy frights have put an end to me.

* [18] They have surrounded me like the waters all the day;
they have encompassed me together.
* [19] Friend and neighbour Thou hast put far from me;
my acquaintance is the darkness.

Psalm 89 (88)

Misericor• ias Domini

The Lord's infallible covenant with David

1 *A Maskil of Ethan the Ezrahite.*

* 2 The mercies of the LORD I will sing forever; †
from generation to generation
I will make known Thy faithfulness with my mouth.
* 3 For I have said, "Mercy shall be built up forever."
Thy faithfulness is established in the heavens.

* 4 "I have made a covenant with My chosen.
I have sworn to David My servant:
* 5 I will establish thy seed forever
and build up thy throne from generation to generation." *Selah*

* 6 The heavens acclaim Thy wonders, O LORD,
Thy faithfulness also, in the church of the holy ones.
* 7 For who in the clouds can be compared to the LORD?
Who is like the LORD among the sons of God?
* 8 A God dreaded in the council of the holy ones,
great and terrible above all round about Him.
* 9 O LORD God of hosts, who is like Thee?
Thou art mighty, O LORD, and Thy faithfulness
surroundeth Thee.

* 10 Thou rulest over the pride of the sea;
when its waves rise up, Thou quietest them.
* 11 Thou didst crush Rahab as one thrust through;
with Thy strong arm, Thou didst scatter Thy enemies.

* 12 The heavens are Thine, the earth also is Thine.
The world and its fulness — Thou hast founded them.
* 13 The north and the south — Thou hast created them;
Tabor and Hermon shout for joy at Thy name.

* [14] Thine is an arm with might;
strong is Thy hand, exalted Thy right hand.
* [15] Justice and judgment are the foundation of Thy throne;
mercy and truth go before Thy face.

* [16] Blessed the people that knoweth the festal cry;
they shall walk, O LORD, in the light of Thy countenance.
* [17] In Thy name will they exult all the day,
and in Thy justice will they be exalted.

* [18] For Thou art the beauty of their strength,
and in Thy good pleasure shall our horn be exalted.
* [19] For our shield belongeth to the LORD,
our king to the Holy One of Israel.

* [20] Then Thou spokest in a vision
to Thy saints, and didst say:
* "I have given help to a mighty man;
I have exalted one chosen from the people.
* [21] I have found David My servant;
with My holy oil I have anointed him,
* [22] so that My hand shall be established with him,
and My arm also shall make him firm.

* [23] The enemy shall not exploit him,
nor the son of injustice humble him.
* [24] And I will beat fine his adversaries before his face,
and smite those that hate him.
* [25] And My faithfulness and My mercy shall be with him,
and in My name shall his horn be exalted.
* [26] And I will put his hand on the sea,
and his right hand upon the rivers.

* [27] He shall call to Me, 'Thou art my father,
my God and the rock of my salvation.'
* [28] And so I will make him the firstborn,
the highest of the kings of the earth.
* [29] I will keep My mercy for him forever,
and My covenant will be faithful for him.

* 30 And I will set firm his seed forever
and his throne as the days of heaven.

* 31 If his children forsake My law
and walk not in My judgments,
* 32 if they profane My statutes
and keep not My commandments,
* 33 then I will visit their transgression with a rod
and their iniquity with blows.

* 34 But My mercy I will not break off from him,
or be false to My faithfulness.
* 35 I will not profane My covenant,
or alter what went forth from My lips.
* 36 Once have I sworn by My holiness:
I will not lie to David.
* 37 His seed shall be forever,
and his throne as the sun before Me.
* 38 As the moon it shall be established forever,
and a faithful witness in heaven." *Selah*

* 39 But Thou hast cast off and rejected,
Thou hast become enraged with Thy anointed.
* 40 Thou hast spurned the covenant of Thy servant;
Thou hast profaned his diadem to the ground.

* 41 Thou hast breached all his walls;
Thou hast laid his fortresses in ruins.
* 42 All that pass by the way despoil him;
he hath become a reproach to his neighbours.
* 43 Thou hast exalted the right hand of his adversaries;
Thou hast made all his enemies rejoice.
* 44 Thou even turnest back the edge of his sword,
and hast not made him stand in battle.

* 45 Thou hast made his splendour to cease;
Thou hast cast his throne to the ground.
* 46 Thou hast shortened the days of his youth;
Thou hast covered him with shame. *Selah*

* [47] How long, O LORD? Wilt Thou hide forever?
Must Thy wrath go on burning like a fire?
* [48] Remember what my lifetime is,
for what vanity Thou hast created all the children of men.
* [49] What man shall live and not see death?
Who shall deliver his soul from the hand of hell? *Selah*

* [50] Where are Thy ancient mercies, O Lord,
which Thou didst swear to David in Thy faithfulness?
* [51] Remember, O Lord, the reproach of Thy servants,
which I bear in my bosom from so many peoples,
* [52] with which Thy enemies have reproached, O LORD,
with which they have reproached the footsteps
of Thy anointed.

* [53] Blessed be the LORD forever.
Amen and amen.

BOOK IV

Psalms 90-106

(The Babylonian exile)

Psalm 90 (89)

Domine, refugium

The eternal God, a shelter for wayfaring man *(homo viator)*

1 *A Prayer of Moses, the man of God.*

* O Lord, Thou hast been our dwelling place
from generation to generation.
* 2 Before the mountains were born, †
or Thou didst bring the earth and the world to birth,
from everlasting to everlasting Thou art God.

* 3 Thou returnest man into dust,
saying, "Return, O children of men."
* 4 For a thousand years in Thy sight, †
are as yesterday when it is past,
and as a watch in the night.

* 5 Thou sweepest them away; †
they are as a night of sleep in the morning.
They are like grass that is renewed:
* 6 in the morning it will blossom and be renewed;
in the evening it will wither and dry up.

* 7 So we are brought to an end by Thy anger,
and by Thy wrath we are dismayed.

* [8] Thou hast set our iniquities before Thee,
our secrets in the light of Thy countenance.

* [9] For all our days decline in Thy wrath;
we bring our years to an end like a sigh.
* [10] The days of our years are threescore years and ten,
or even, by reason of vigour, fourscore years;
* and their greater part are toil and trouble,
for they pass hastily, and we fly away.
* [11] Who knoweth the strength of Thy anger,
and Thy wrath, according to the fear of Thee?

* [12] Teach us so to number our days
that we may get a heart of wisdom.
* [13] Return, O LORD — how long?
And have pity upon Thy servants.

* [14] Satisfy us in the morning with Thy mercy,
and we shall cry aloud and rejoice all our days.
* [15] Make us glad according to the days when Thou didst humble us,
the years when we saw evil.

* [16] Let Thy work appear to Thy servants,
and Thy splendour be upon their children.
* [17] And let the sweetness of the Lord our God be upon us; †
and the work of our hands establish for us,
indeed, establish the work of our hands.

Psalm 91 (90)

Qui habitat

"In tribulation I will be with him"

* 1 He that dwelleth in the covert of the Most High
shall abide in the shadow of the Almighty.
* 2 He shall say to the LORD, "My refuge and my fortress;
my God, in Him will I trust."

* 3 For He will deliver thee from the snare of the fowler,
and from the ruinous pestilence.
* 4 He will cover thee with His pinions, †
and under His wings thou shalt take refuge;
His truth is a shield and a buckler.

* 5 Thou shalt not be afraid of the terror of the night,
of the arrow that flieth by day,
* 6 of the pestilence that walketh in the darkness,
of the destroyer that devastateth at noonday.

* 7 A thousand shall fall at thy side, †
and ten thousand at thy right hand,
but it shall not come near to thee.
* 8 Thou shalt only look with thy eyes
and see the retribution of the wicked.

* 9 Because thou hast said, "The LORD is my refuge,"
thou hast made the Most High thy habitation.
* 10 No evil shall befall thee,
no scourge come near thy tent.

* 11 For He will command His angels concerning thee
to keep thee in all thy ways.
* 12 On their hands they shall bear thee up,
lest thou dash thy foot against a stone.
* 13 Thou shalt tread on the asp and the viper;
thou shalt trample the lion and the dragon.

* 14 "Because he hath cleaved to Me, I will deliver him;
I will set him on high, because he hath known My name.
* 15 When he shall call to Me, I will answer him; †
in tribulation I will be with him;
I will deliver him and glorify him.
* 16 With length of days I will satisfy him,
and shew him My salvation."

Psalm 92 (91)

Bonum est confiteri

The very deep devices of Providence

1 *A Psalm. A Song for the Sabbath Day.*

* 2 It is good to give thanks to the LORD,
and to sing psalms to Thy name, O Most High;
* 3 to declare Thy mercy in the morning,
and Thy faithfulness by night,
* 4 on the instrument of ten strings and on the psaltery,
with music upon the harp.

* 5 For Thou hast made me glad by Thy deeds, O LORD;
at the works of Thy hands I shout for joy.
* 6 How great are Thy works, O LORD;
very deep are Thy designs.
* 7 A brutish man will not know,
nor a fool understand this.

* 8 When the wicked flourish like herbage,
and all wrongdoers blossom,
* they are due to be destroyed forever,
9 but Thou, O LORD, art on high forever.
* 10 For lo, Thy enemies, O LORD, †
for lo, Thy enemies shall perish,
all wrongdoers shall be scattered.

* [11] But Thou hast exalted my horn like the wild ox;
I am anointed with fresh oil.
* [12] And my eyes shall gaze upon my adversaries,
my ears shall hear of the evildoers that assailed me.

* [13] The just shall flourish like the palm tree;
like a cedar in Lebanon shall he grow.

* [14] They that are planted in the house of the LORD
shall flourish in the courts of our God.
* [15] They still bear fruit in old age;
fat and luxuriant shall they be,
* [16] to declare that the LORD is upright —
my rock, and there is no unrighteousness in Him.

Psalm 93 (92)

Dominus regnavit

Creation, the Lord's vesture and dominion

* [1] The LORD reigneth; He is robed in majesty.
The LORD is robed; He hath girded Himself with strength.
* Indeed, the world is established, it shall not be moved; †
[2] Thy throne is established from of old;
Thou art from everlasting.

* [3] The floods have lifted up, O LORD, †
the floods have lifted up their voice;
the floods have lifted up their pounding.
* [4] More than the voice of many waters, †
more magnificent than the breakers of the sea,
the LORD is magnificent on high.

* [5] Thy testimonies are very sure. †
Holiness becometh Thy house,
O LORD, for length of days.

Psalm 94 (93)

Deus ultionum

"Vengeance is Mine; I will repay" (Hebrews 10:30)

* 1 O Lord, God of vengeance,
O God of vengeance, shine forth.
* 2 Lift up Thyself, O judge of the earth;
render a recompense to the proud.

* 3 How long shall the wicked, O LORD,
how long shall the wicked exult?
* 4 They pour forth insolent speech;
all the wrongdoers vaunt themselves.

* 5 They crush Thy people, O LORD,
and humble Thy inheritance.
* 6 They slay the widow and the stranger,
and murder the fatherless.

* 7 And they have said, "The LORD will not see,
nor will the God of Jacob understand."
* 8 Understand, ye brutish among the people;
and ye fools, when will you have insight?
* 9 He that planted the ear, shall He not hear,
or He that formed the eye, shall He not look?
* 10 He that disciplineth nations, shall He not rebuke —
He that teacheth man knowledge?
* 11 The LORD knoweth the devices of man,
that they are vanity.

* 12 Blessed the man whom Thou shalt discipline, O LORD,
and shalt teach out of Thy law,
* 13 to give him rest from evil days,
until a pit be dug for the wicked.

* 14 For the LORD will not abandon His people,
nor forsake His inheritance.

* 15 For judgment shall return to the just,
and all the upright of heart shall follow it.

* 16 Who will rise up for me against the evildoers?
Who will take a stand for me against the wrongdoers?
* 17 Unless the LORD had been my help,
my soul would soon have dwelt in silence.

* 18 If I say, "My foot is moved,"
Thy mercy, O LORD, will uphold me.
* 19 When cares are many within me,
Thy consolations delight my soul.

* 20 Can a throne of ruin be allied with Thee,
framing mischief by statute?
* 21 They band together against the soul of the just,
and condemn innocent blood.

* 22 But the LORD hath become a high place for me,
and my God the rock of my refuge.
* 23 And He will bring back on them their iniquity, †
and destroy them in their evil;
24 the LORD our God will destroy them.

Psalm 95 (94)

Venite, exultemus

"He demarcates a certain day, *today*" (Hebrews 4:7; cf. v.8)

* 1 O come, ring out our joy to the LORD;
make jubilation to the rock of our salvation.
* 2 Let us come before His face with thanksgiving;
with psalms, let us make jubilee to Him.

* 3 For the LORD is a great God,
and a great king above all gods.
* 4 In His hands are the depths of the earth,
and the heights of the mountains are His.
* 5 The sea is His, and He made it,
and His hands formed the dry land.

* 6 O come let us adore and bow down;
let us kneel before the LORD Who made us.
* 7 For He is our God, †
and we are the people of His pasture
and the sheep of His hand.

* 8 "Today if you shall hear His voice,
harden not your hearts, as at Meribah,
* 9 as on the day of Massah in the wilderness, †
where your fathers tempted Me.
They proved Me, though they saw My works.

* 10 For forty years I loathed that generation, †
and I said, 'They are a people who err in heart,
and they have not known My ways.'
* 11 Therefore I swore in My anger:
'They shall not enter into My rest.' "

Psalm 96 (95)

Cantate Domino

"Evangelize His salvation from day to day" (v.2b, Greek)

* 1 O sing to the LORD a new song; †
Sing to the LORD all the earth.
2 Sing to the LORD, bless His name.

* Tell the good tidings of His salvation from day to day; †
3 declare among the Gentiles His glory,
among all the peoples His wonders.

* 4 For great is the LORD, and exceedingly to be praised;
He is to be feared above all gods.
* 5 For all the gods of the peoples are things of naught,
but the LORD made the heavens.

* 6 Majesty and splendour are before Him;
strength and beauty are in His sanctuary.

* 7 Ascribe to the LORD, O families of peoples, †
ascribe to the LORD glory and strength.
8 Ascribe to the LORD the glory of His name.

* Bring an offering and enter His courts. †
9 Adore the LORD in holy splendour;
tremble before Him, all the earth.

* 10 Say among the Gentiles, "The LORD reigneth. †
Indeed, the world is established, it shall not be moved;
He will judge the peoples with equity."

* 11 Let the heavens be glad and the earth exult;
let the sea thunder and the fulness thereof;
* 12 let the field be overjoyed and all that is in it;
then shall all the trees of the wood ring out their joy:

* 13 Before the face of the LORD, because He cometh,
because He cometh to judge the earth.
* He will judge the world with justice,
and the peoples in His faithfulness.

Psalm 97 (96)

Dominus regnavit

"He will come again in glory to judge the living and the dead"
(Nicene Creed)

* 1 The LORD reigneth; let the earth exult;
let the many islands be glad.
* 2 Cloud and gloom are round about Him;
justice and judgment are the foundation of His throne.

* 3 Fire shall go before Him,
and burn up His adversaries round about.
* 4 His lightings lighted up the world;
the earth saw and trembled.
* 5 The mountains melted like wax before the LORD,
before the Lord of all the earth.
* 6 The heavens declared His justice,
and all peoples saw His glory.

* 7 Let all that serve graven things be ashamed, †
those that boast of things of naught.
Adore Him, all ye gods.

* 8 Zion heard and was glad, †
and the daughters of Judah exulted,
because of Thy judgments, O LORD.
* 9 For Thou, O LORD, †
art most high over all the earth;
Thou art exalted far above all gods.

* 10 You that love the LORD, hate evil! †
He keepeth the souls of His saints;
He will deliver them from the hand of the wicked.

* 11 Light is sown for the just,
and joy for the upright of heart.
* 12 Rejoice, ye just, in the LORD,
and give thanks to the remembrance of His holiness.

Psalm 98 (97)

Cantate Domino

All offered salvation, all to be judged (cf. Acts 17:30-31)

1 *A Psalm.*

* O sing to the LORD a new song,
for He hath done marvelous things.
* His right hand hath wrought for Him salvation,
and His holy arm.

* 2 The LORD hath made known His salvation;
in the sight of the Gentiles, He hath revealed His justice.
* 3 He hath remembered His mercy and His faithfulness
to the house of Israel.
* All the ends of the earth have seen
the salvation of our God.
* 4 Make jubilation to the LORD all the earth;
break forth and ring out and sing a psalm.

* 5 Sing a psalm to the LORD with the harp,
with the harp and the voice of a psalm.
* 6 With trumpets and the sound of the horn,
make jubilation before the King, the LORD.

* 7 Let the sea thunder, and the fulness thereof,
the world and they that dwell therein.
* 8 Let the rivers clap their hands;
let the hills ring out together
* 9 before the face of the LORD,
for He cometh to judge the earth.
* He will judge the world with justice,
and the peoples with equity.

Psalm 99 (98)

Dominus regnavit

"I am holy" (Leviticus 11:44)

* 1 The LORD reigneth; let the peoples tremble.
He sitteth upon the cherubim; let the earth quake.
* 2 The LORD is great in Zion,
and He is exalted over all the peoples.

* 3 Let them confess Thy name, great and terrible:
Holy is He.

* 4 And with kingly strength He loveth judgment. †
Thou hast established equity;
Thou hast wrought judgment and justice in Jacob.

* 5 Exalt ye the LORD our God, †
and adore at His footstool:
Holy is He.

* 6 Moses and Aaron were among His priests, †
and Samuel among those that called upon His name.
They called upon the LORD, and He answered them.
* 7 He spoke to them in the pillar of cloud.
They kept His testimonies and the statute that He gave them.

* 8 O LORD, our God, Thou didst answer them; †
Thou wast a forgiving God to them,
but an avenger of their misdeeds.

* 9 Exalt ye the LORD our God, †
and adore at His holy mountain;
for holy is the LORD our God.

Psalm 100 (99)

Jubilate Deo

The Tetragrammaton: "The Lord (YHWH), *He* is God"

(Catechism of the Catholic Church 206, 209, 213)

1 *A Psalm for the thank-offering.*

* 2 Make jubilation to the LORD, all the earth. †
Serve the LORD with gladness;
come before Him ringing out your joy.

* 3 Know ye that the LORD, He is God; †
He made us, and His we are,
His people, and the sheep of His pasture.

* 4 Enter into His gates with thanksgiving, †
into His courts with praise;
give thanks to Him, bless His name.

* 5 For the LORD is good; †
His mercy is everlasting,
and His faithfulness from generation to generation.

Psalm 101 (100)

Misericor•iam et ju•icium

"Bad company corrupts good morals" (1 Corinthians 15:33)

1 *A Psalm of Davi•.*

* I will sing of mercy and judgment;
to Thee, O LORD, will I sing a psalm.
* 2 I will study the way of integrity;
when wilt Thou come to me?

* I will walk in the integrity of my heart
within my house.
* 3 I will not set before my eyes
any worthless thing.

* I hate the doing of the devious;
it shall not cleave to me.
* 4 A perverse heart shall depart from me;
I will not know evil.

* 5 One who slandereth his neighbour in secret
I will put to an end;
* the haughty of eyes and the arrogant of heart
I cannot bear.

* 6 My eyes are on the faithful of the land,
that they may dwell with me.
* He who walketh in the way of integrity
shall minister to me.

* 7 No one who worketh deceit
shall abide within my house;
* no one who speaketh falsehood
shall be established before my eyes.

* 8 Morning by morning I will put to an end
all the wicked of the land,
* to cut off from the city of the LORD
all the wrongdoers.

Psalm 102 (101)

Domine, exaudi

The perishing of Zion beseech the Everlasting

(Fifth Penitential Psalm)

[1] *A prayer of the afflicted, who is faint and poureth out his concern before the LORD.*

* [2] O LORD, hear my prayer,
and let my cry come unto Thee.
* [3] Hide not Thy face from me
in the day of my distress.
* Incline Thy ear to me;
in the day when I call, make haste to answer me.

* [4] For my days have vanished like smoke,
and my bones burn like a hearth.
* [5] My heart is stricken like the grass and withered,
for I forget to eat my bread.
* [6] At the voice of my groaning,
my bones have cleaved to my flesh.

* [7] I have become like a pelican of the wilderness,
like an owl among the ruins.
* [8] I watch, and I have been
like a sparrow all alone on the housetop.
* [9] All the day have my enemies reproached me;
those that make a fool of me swear at me.

* [10] For I have eaten ashes like bread,
and mingled my drink with weeping,
* [11] because of Thy indignation and Thy fury,
for Thou hast lifted me up and thrown me down.
* [12] My days are like a lengthening shadow,
and I wither like the grass.

* [13] But Thou, O LORD, abidest forever,
and Thy memorial from generation to generation.

* 14 Thou shalt arise and have compassion on Zion, †
for it is time to be gracious to her,
for the appointed time hath come.
* 15 For Thy servants take pleasure in her stones,
and feel pity for her dust.

* 16 And the nations shall fear Thy name, O LORD,
and all the kings of the earth Thy glory,
* 17 when the LORD hath built up Zion,
and appeared in His glory;
* 18 when He hath turned to the prayer of the destitute,
and not despised their supplication.

* 19 Let this be written for a generation to come,
that a people yet to be created may praise the LORD:
* 20 that He looked down from the height of His sanctuary,
from heaven the LORD looked upon the earth,
* 21 to hear the groaning of the prisoners,
to loose those doomed to death;
* 22 that the name of the LORD may be declared in Zion
and His praise in Jerusalem,
* 23 when peoples gather together,
and kingdoms, to serve the LORD.

* 24 He hath humbled my strength in the way;
He hath shortened my days.
* I say, "O my God, †
25 take me not away in the midst of my days.
Thy years are throughout all generations."

* 26 In the beginning Thou didst found the earth,
and the heavens are the work of Thy hands.
* 27 They shall perish, but Thou shalt remain,
and they shall all grow old like a garment;
* Thou shalt change them like clothing, and they shall
be changed,
28 but Thou art the selfsame, and Thy years shall not end.

* 29 The children of Thy servants shall continue,
and their seed shall be established before Thee.

Psalm 103 (102)

Benedic, anima mea

Blessing Him Who has blessed us

1 *A Psalm of David.*

* Bless the LORD, O my soul,
and all that is within me, bless His holy name.
* 2 Bless the LORD, O my soul,
and forget not all that He hath done for thee.

* 3 Who forgiveth all thy iniquities,
Who healeth all thy diseases,
* 4 Who redeemeth thy life from destruction,
Who crowneth thee with mercy and compassion,
* 5 Who satisfieth thy lifetime with good things;
thy youth shall be renewed like the eagle's.

* 6 The LORD doth just deeds
and judgments for all that are oppressed.
* 7 He made known His ways to Moses,
His acts to the children of Israel.

* 8 The LORD is compassionate and gracious,
slow to anger and plenteous in mercy.
* 9 He will not always contend,
nor will He be angry forever.
* 10 He hath not dealt with us according to our sins,
nor requited us according to our iniquities.

* 11 For as heaven is high above the earth,
so strong is His mercy upon those that fear Him.
* 12 As far as the east is from the west,
so far hath He removed our transgressions from us.

* 13 As a father hath compassion on his children,
so the LORD hath compassion on those that fear Him.
* 14 For He knoweth our frame;
He remembereth that we are dust.

* [15] Man's days are as grass;
as a flower of the field, so shall he flourish;
* [16] for the wind passeth over it, and it is no more,
and its place knoweth it no longer.

* [17] But the mercy of the LORD is from everlasting to everlasting
upon those that fear Him,
* and His justice unto children's children, †
[18] for those that keep His covenant
and are mindful of His precepts, to do them.

* [19] The LORD hath established His throne in heaven,
and His kingdom ruleth over all.
* [20] Bless the LORD, O ye His angels, †
mighty in power, that do His word,
hearkening to the voice of His word.
* [21] Bless the LORD, all ye His hosts,
His ministers that do His will.
* [22] Bless the LORD, all His works, †
in every place of His dominion.
Bless the LORD, O my soul.

Psalm 104 (103)

Bene•ic, anima mea

"Majesty and splendour": The glory of the Hexameron (Genesis 1)

* 1 Bless the LORD, O my soul.
O LORD my God, Thou art very great.
* Thou hast put on majesty and splendour,
2 wrapping Thyself with light as with a mantle.

* Who stretchest out the heavens like a tent-cloth,
3 Who layeth the beams of His upper chambers upon the waters,
* Who maketh the clouds His chariot,
Who rideth upon the wings of the wind,
* 4 Who maketh His angels winds,
and His ministers flaming fire.

* 5 Who founded the earth on its foundations,
that it might never be moved.
* 6 The deep covered it as a garment;
the waters stood above the mountains.
* 7 At Thy rebuke, they fled;
at the voice of Thy thunder, they hastened away.
* 8 The mountains rose up, the valleys sank down,
to the place which Thou didst found for them.
* Thou didst set a bound that they shall not pass;
9 they shall not return to cover the earth.

* 10 Who sendeth forth springs into the watercourses;
they run between the hills.
* 11 They give drink to all the beasts of the field;
the wild asses quench their thirst.
* 12 Beside them dwell the birds of heaven;
from among the branches they give voice.

* 13 Who watereth the mountains from His upper chambers;
the earth is satisfied with the fruit of Thy works.

* 14 Making grass spring up for the cattle,
and plants for the service of man;
* to bring forth bread from the earth,
15 and wine that maketh glad the heart of man,
* to make his face shine with oil,
and bread that sustaineth man's heart.

* 16 The trees of the LORD get their fill,
the cedars of Lebanon which He planted.
* 17 There the birds build their nests;
the stork has the fir trees for her house;
* 18 the high mountains are for the wild goats;
the rocks are a refuge for the conies.

* 19 He made the moon for the seasons;
the sun knoweth its going down.
* 20 Thou makest darkness, and it is night,
wherein all the beasts of the forest creep about;
* 21 the young lions roar for prey,
seeking their food from God.
* 22 The sun ariseth, and they gather together
and go to lie down in their dens.
* 23 Man goeth forth to his work,
and to his labour until evening.

* 24 How many are Thy works, O LORD. †
All of them Thou hast made in wisdom;
the earth is full of Thy creatures.
* 25 Here is the sea, great and spreading wide, †
wherein are creeping things innumerable,
living things both little and great.
* 26 There go the ships;
there is Leviathan, which Thou didst form to sport with.

* 27 All of them look expectantly unto Thee,
to give them their food in due season.

* [28] When Thou givest it to them, they shall gather it up;
when Thou openest Thy hand, they shall be satisfied
with good.

* [29] When Thou turnest away Thy face, they shall be dismayed; †
when Thou takest away their spirit, they shall expire
and return to their dust.

* [30] Thou shalt send forth Thy Spirit, and they shall be created,
and Thou shalt renew the face of the earth.

* [31] May the glory of the LORD be forever.
May the LORD rejoice in His works,

* [32] Who looketh at the earth and it trembleth,
Who toucheth the mountains and they smoke.

* [33] I will sing to the LORD while I live;
I will sing psalms to my God while I have my being.

* [34] May my meditation be pleasing to Him;
I will rejoice in the LORD.

* [35] Let sinners cease from the earth,
and let the wicked be no more.

* Bless the LORD, O my soul.
Alleluia.

Psalm 105 (104)

Confitemini Domino

The Lord, the covenant keeper

* 1 Give thanks to the LORD, †
call upon His name,
make known His deeds among the peoples.
* 2 Sing to Him, chant a psalm to Him,
meditate on all His wonders.
* 3 Boast in His holy name;
let the heart of them that seek the LORD rejoice.

* 4 Seek ye the LORD and His strength;
seek His face without ceasing.
* 5 Remember His wonders that He hath done,
His portents, and the judgments of His mouth.

* 6 O ye seed of Abraham His servant,
ye children of Jacob His chosen,
* 7 He is the LORD our God:
His judgments are in all the earth.

* 8 He hath remembered His covenant forever,
the word that He commanded for a thousand generations,
* 9 which He made with Abraham,
and His oath to Isaac.
* 10 And He established it for Jacob as a statute,
and for Israel as an everlasting covenant,
* 11 saying, "To thee will I give the land of Canaan,
the lot of your inheritance."

* 12 When they were but a few men in number,
very few, and strangers in it,
* 13 and went about from nation to nation,
and from one kingdom to another people,
* 14 He let no man oppress them,
and rebuked kings for their sake:

* 15 "Touch not My anointed ones,
and to My prophets do no harm."

* 16 And He called a famine upon the land;
He broke every staff of bread.
* 17 He sent a man before them:
Joseph was sold for a slave.
* 18 They humbled his feet with fetters;
his neck entered into iron.
* 19 Until the time that his word came to pass,
the word of the LORD refined him.
* 20 The king sent and loosed him,
even the ruler of the peoples, and released him.
* 21 He made him lord of his house,
and ruler of all his possessions,
* 22 to discipline his princes at will,
and to teach his elders wisdom.

* 23 Then Israel went into Egypt,
and Jacob sojourned in the land of Ham.
* 24 And He made His people very fruitful,
and He made them stronger than their adversaries.
* 25 He turned their heart to hate His people,
and to deal craftily with His servants.

* 26 He sent Moses His servant,
Aaron, whom He had chosen.
* 27 They set among them the words of His signs,
and portents in the land of Ham.

* 28 He sent darkness, and it grew dark,
but they rebelled against His words.
* 29 He turned their waters into blood,
and caused their fish to die.
* 30 Their land teemed with frogs,
into the inner chambers of their kings.
* 31 He spoke, and there came swarms of flies,
and gnats in all their borders.

* 32 He gave them hail for rain,
flaming fire in their land.
* 33 And He struck their vines and fig trees,
and shattered the trees in their borders.
* 34 He spoke, and the locust came,
and the young locust, of which there was no number,
* 35 and they ate up all the foliage in their land,
and they ate up the fruit of their ground.

* 36 And He struck all the firstborn in their land,
the firstfruits of all their vigour.
* 37 And He brought them out with silver and gold,
and there was none among His tribes that stumbled.
* 38 Egypt was glad when they departed,
for dread of them had fallen upon them.

* 39 He spread a cloud for a screen,
and fire to give light by night.
* 40 They asked, and He brought quail,
and He satisfied them with the bread of heaven.
* 41 He opened the rock, and water gushed out;
it ran in the parched places like a river.

* 42 For He remembered His holy word,
to Abraham His servant.
* 43 And He brought forth His people with joy,
His chosen ones with ringing cries.

* 44 And He gave them the lands of the Gentiles,
and they possessed the toil of the peoples,
* 45 that they might keep His statutes,
and observe His laws. Alleluia.

Psalm 106 (105)

Confitemini Domino

"They waited not for His counsel"

* 1 Alleluia. †
O give thanks to the LORD, for He is good,
for His mercy is everlasting.

* 2 Who can utter the mighty acts of the LORD,
or make heard all His praise?
* 3 Blessed are they that keep judgment,
that do justice at all times.

* 4 Remember me, O LORD, †
in Thy good will toward Thy people;
visit me with Thy salvation;
* 5 that I may see the good things of Thy chosen, †
that I may rejoice in the joy of Thy nation,
that I may boast with Thy inheritance.

* 6 We have sinned, together with our fathers;
we have committed iniquity, we have done wickedly.
* 7 Our fathers in Egypt
perceived not Thy wonderful works.
* They remembered not the multitude of Thy mercies,
but rebelled beside the sea, at the Red Sea.
* 8 Yet He saved them for His name's sake,
that He might make known His power.

* 9 And He rebuked the Red Sea, and it dried up,
and He led them through the depths as through a wilderness.
* 10 And He saved them from the hand of him that hated them,
and He redeemed them from the hand of the enemy.
* 11 And the waters covered their adversaries;
there was not one of them left.
* 12 Then they believed His words;
they sang His praise.

* 13 Quickly they forgot His works;
they waited not for His counsel.
* 14 And they conceived a craving in the wilderness,
and tempted God in the wasteland.
* 15 So He gave them their request,
but sent emaciation into their souls.

* 16 In the camp they were jealous of Moses
and of Aaron, the holy one of the LORD.
* 17 The earth opened and swallowed up Dathan,
and covered the company of Abiram.
* 18 And a fire was kindled in their company;
the flame burned up the wicked.

* 19 They made a calf at Horeb
and adored a molten image;
* 20 so they exchanged their glory
for the likeness of an ox that eateth grass.
* 21 They forgot God Who had saved them,
Who had done great things in Egypt,
* 22 wondrous things in the land of Ham,
terrible things at the Red Sea.
* 23 Therefore He said He would do away with them,
had not Moses, His chosen,
* stood in the breach before Him,
to turn away His wrath from destroying them.

* 24 And they refused the desirable land;
they believed not His word.
* 25 And they murmured in their tents;
they hearkened not to the voice of the LORD.
* 26 Therefore He lifted up His hand against them
to make them fall in the wilderness,
* 27 and to make their seed fall among the Gentiles,
and to scatter them in the lands.

* 28 They also yoked themselves to the Baal of Peor,
and ate the sacrifices of the dead;

* 29 thus they provoked Him with their deeds,
and a plague broke out among them.
* 30 Then Phinehas stood and executed judgment,
and the plague was stayed,
* 31 and it was reckoned to him as justice
from generation to generation forever.

* 32 They angered Him also at the waters of Meribah,
and it went ill with Moses because of them;
* 33 for they embittered his spirit,
and he spoke rashly with his lips.

* 34 They did not do away with the peoples,
as the LORD had said to them,
* 35 but they mingled with the heathen
and learned their works.
* 36 So they served their idols,
and they became a snare to them.
* 37 They even sacrificed their sons
and their daughters to the demons.
* 38 And they poured out innocent blood,
the blood of their sons and of their daughters,
* whom they sacrificed to the idols of Canaan;
and the land was defiled with blood.

* 39 So they became unclean by their works,
and practiced fornication in their deeds.
* 40 Therefore the anger of the LORD was kindled against
His people,
and He abhorred His inheritance.
* 41 And He gave them into the hand of the nations,
and those that hated them ruled over them.
* 42 So their enemies oppressed them,
and they were humbled under their hand.

* 43 Many times He delivered them, †
but they rebelled in their counsel,
and sank low through their iniquity.

* [44] Yet He looked upon their distress,
when He heard their outcry.

* [45] And He remembered His covenant with them,
and repented according to the abundance of His mercy.
* [46] And He gave them over to find pity
in the sight of all that held them captive.

* [47] Save us, O LORD our God,
and gather us from among the nations,
* that we may give thanks to Thy holy name,
that we may boast in Thy praise.

* [48] Blessed be the LORD, the God of Israel,
from everlasting and unto everlasting.
* And let all the people say:
"Amen, Alleluia."

BOOK V

Psalms 107-150

(The restoration of Zion)

Psalm 107 (106)

Confitemini Domino

The Lord will deliver His suppliants from every calamity

* 1 O give thanks to the LORD, for He is good,
for His mercy is everlasting.

* 2 Let the redeemed of the LORD say so,
whom He redeemed from the hand of the adversary,
* 3 and gathered them out of the lands, †
from the rising and from the setting of the sun,
from the north and from the sea.

* 4 They wandered in the wilderness, in a wasteland;
they found no way to an inhabitable city.
* 5 Hungry and thirsty,
their soul fainted within them.
* 6 And they cried to the LORD in their tribulation,
and from their straits He delivered them.
* 7 And He led them by a straight way
to go to an inhabitable city.

* 8 Let them give thanks to the LORD for His mercy,
and for His wondrous works to the children of men,
* 9 for He hath satisfied the thirsty soul,
and the hungry soul He hath filled with good things.

* 10 Such as sat in darkness and the shadow of death
were prisoners in affliction and in iron,
* 11 for they had rebelled against the words of God,
and spurned the counsel of the Most High.
* 12 So He humbled their heart with labour;
they stumbled, and there was none to help.
* 13 And they cried to the LORD in their tribulation,
and from their straits He saved them.
* 14 He brought them out of darkness and the shadow of death,
and broke their bonds asunder.

* 15 Let them give thanks to the LORD for His mercy,
and for His wondrous works to the children of men,
* 16 for He hath shattered the doors of bronze,
and hacked off the bars of iron.

* 17 Fools, through the way of their transgression,
and through their iniquities brought affliction on themselves.
* 18 Their soul abhorred every kind of food,
and they drew near to the gates of death.
* 19 And they cried to the LORD in their tribulation,
and from their straits He saved them.
* 20 He sent forth His word and healed them,
and delivered them from their destruction.

* 21 Let them give thanks to the LORD for His mercy,
and for His wondrous works to the children of men.
* 22 And let them offer sacrifices of thanksgiving,
and tell of His works with ringing cries.

* 23 They that go down to the sea in ships,
doing business in the great waters,
* 24 these have seen the works of the LORD,
and His wonders in the deep.
* 25 For He spoke and raised up the stormy wind,
and it lifted up its waves.
* 26 They mounted up to heaven and went down to the depths;
their soul melted away because of the evil.

* [27] They reeled and staggered like a drunken man,
and all their wisdom was swallowed up.
* [28] And they cried to the LORD in their tribulation,
and from their straits He delivered them.
* [29] He turned the storm into a whisper,
and the waves of it were hushed.
* [30] Then they rejoiced because they had calm,
and He led them to their desired haven.

* [31] Let them give thanks to the LORD for His mercy,
and for His wondrous works to the children of men.
* [32] And let them exalt Him in the church of the people,
and praise Him in the session of the elders.

* [33] He turned rivers into a wilderness,
and springs of water into thirsty ground,
* [34] a fruitful land into a salt waste,
because of the evil of its inhabitants.

* [35] He turned a wilderness into pools of water,
and a parched land into springs of water,
* [36] and He settled the hungry there,
and they established an inhabitable city.
* [37] And they sowed fields and planted vineyards,
and these produced a fruitful yield.
* [38] He also blessed them, so that they multiplied greatly,
and He let not their cattle diminish.

* [39] When they diminished and were brought low
from oppression, evil, and sorrow,
* [40] He poured contempt upon princes
and made them wander in a pathless waste.
* [41] But He set on high the needy from affliction,
and made families like a flock.
* [42] Let the upright see it and rejoice,
and all injustice shut its mouth.

* [43] Whoever is wise, let him keep these things,
and let men understand the mercies of the LORD.

Psalm 108 (107)

Paratum cor meum

Ardent praise, and perseverance in the face of failure

1 *A Song. A Psalm of David.*

* 2 My heart is steadfast, O God. †
I will sing and chant a psalm,
even to Thee, my glory.
* 3 Awake, O psaltery and harp;
I will awake the dawn.

* 4 I will confess to Thee, O LORD, among the peoples,
I will sing psalms to Thee among the nations,
* 5 because Thy mercy is great above the heavens,
and Thy truth unto the clouds.

* 6 Be exalted above the heavens, O God,
and over all the earth be Thy glory.

* 7 That Thy beloved may be delivered,
save with Thy right hand, and answer me.

* 8 God hath spoken in His sanctuary: †
"I will exult, I will divide up Shechem
and mete out the valley of Succoth.
* 9 Gilead is Mine, and Manasseh is Mine,
and Ephraim is the protection of My head;
* Judah is My scepter.
10 Moab is My washbasin;
* upon Edom I will cast My shoe;
over Philistia I will shout for joy."

* 11 Who will bring me into the fortified city?
Who will lead me to Edom?
* 12 Hast not Thou, O God, cast us off?
And Thou goest not forth, O God, with our armies.

* 13 O give us help from trouble,
for vain is the salvation of man.
* 14 In God we shall do valiantly,
and He will tread down our adversaries.

Psalm 109 (108)

Deus, laudem meam

"A prophecy about Judas" (Origen; cf. Acts 1:16, 20)

1 *To the choirmaster. A Psalm of David.*

* O God of my praise, be not silent, †
2 for the mouth of the wicked and the mouth of deceit,
they have opened against me.

* They have spoken to me with a lying tongue, †
3 and surrounded me with words of hatred,
and fought against me without cause.
* 4 In return for my love they accuse me,
but I make my prayer.
* 5 And they have laid upon me evil for good,
and hatred for my love.

* 6 "Appoint a wicked man over him,
and let an accuser stand at his right hand.
* 7 When he is judged, let him go forth condemned,
and let his prayer be accounted sin.
* 8 Let his days become few;
let another take his overseership.

* 9 Let his children become fatherless,
and his wife be a widow.
* 10 And let his children wander about and beg,
and seek a place away from their ruins.
* 11 Let the usurer ensnare all that is his,
and let strangers despoil his labour.
* 12 Let there be none to extend him mercy,
or to be gracious to his fatherless children.
* 13 Let his posterity be cut off;
let their name be blotted out in the next generation.

* 14 Let the iniquities of his fathers be remembered to the LORD,
and let not the sin of his mother be blotted out.

* [15] Let them be before the LORD continually,
to cut off their memory from the earth.

* [16] For he remembered not to do mercy, †
but he persecuted the poor and the needy man
and the brokenhearted, to put him to death.
* [17] For he loved cursing, and so it came to him,
and he wanted not blessing, and so it was far from him.

* [18] Since he put on cursing like a garment, †
so it went into his entrails like water,
and like oil into his bones.
* [19] It shall be for him like a garment that covereth him,
and like a girdle with which he continually girdeth himself."

* [20] This is the retribution of my accusers from the LORD,
and of those who speak evil against my soul.
* [21] But Thou, O LORD, my Lord, †
deal with me for Thy name's sake;
because Thy mercy is good, deliver me.

* [22] For I am poor and needy,
and my heart is wounded within me.
* [23] I am gone like a lengthening shadow;
I am shaken off like a locust.
* [24] My knees totter through fasting,
and my flesh is wasted from want of oil.
* [25] I have become a reproach to them;
when they see me, they wag their heads.

* [26] Help me, O LORD my God,
save me according to Thy mercy.
* [27] And let them know that this is Thy hand,
that Thou, O LORD, hast done it.

* [28] They may curse, but Thou wilt bless. †
Let them that rise up against me be confounded,
but let Thy servant rejoice.

* [29] Let my accusers be clothed with disgrace,
and wrapped in their shame as in a mantle.

* [30] I will give thanks to the LORD exceedingly with my mouth,
and in the midst of many I will praise Him,
* [31] for He standeth at the right hand of the needy,
to save him from them that judge his soul.

Psalm 110 (109)

Dixit Dominus

"David himself calls him Lord" (Mark 12:37)

[1] *A Psalm of David.*

* The LORD said to my Lord: †
"Sit at My right hand,
until I make thy enemies thy footstool."

* [2] The scepter of thy strength †
the LORD will send forth from Zion:
Rule in the midst of thy enemies!

* [3] With thee is the principality
on the day of thy birth:
* In holy splendour, from the womb of the dawn,
like the dew I have begotten thee.

* [4] The LORD hath sworn, and He will not repent: †
"Thou art a priest forever
according to the order of Melchizedek."

* [5] The Lord at thy right hand
shall smite kings on the day of His anger.
* [6] He shall judge among the nations; †
He will fill them with corpses;
He will smite heads over the wide earth.

* [7] He shall drink from the brook in the way;
therefore shall he lift up his head.

Psalm 111 (110)

Confitebor tibi, Domine

"A memorial of His wonders": the Passover and the Mass

* 1 Alleluia. †
I will confess to the LORD with all my heart,
in the council of the upright, and in the congregation.
* 2 Great are the works of the LORD,
to be sought out by all who desire them.

* 3 Majesty and splendour is His work,
and His justice abideth forever.
* 4 He hath made a memorial of His wonders;
gracious and compassionate is the LORD.

* 5 He hath given food to those who fear Him;
He will be mindful forever of His covenant.
* 6 He hath shown His people the power of His works,
by giving them the inheritance of the nations.

* 7 The works of His hands are truth and judgment;
all His precepts are faithful.
* 8 They are upheld forever and ever,
to be done in truth and equity.

* 9 He hath sent redemption to His people; †
He hath commanded His covenant forever.
Holy and terrible is His name.

* 10 The fear of the LORD is the beginning of wisdom. †
Good insight have all that do them.
His praise abideth forever.

Psalm 112 (111)

Beatus vir

"He dispersed, he gave to the needy; his justice abides forever"
(2 Corinthians 9:9)

* 1 Alleluia. †
Blessed is the man who feareth the LORD,
who greatly desireth His commandments.
* 2 His seed shall be mighty in the land;
the generation of the upright shall be blessed.

* 3 Wealth and riches are in his house,
and his justice abideth forever.
* 4 Light dawneth in the darkness for the upright;
he is gracious and compassionate and just.

* 5 It is well with the man who dealeth graciously and lendeth,
who shall manage his affairs with judgment.
* 6 For he shall never be moved;
the just shall be in everlasting remembrance.

* 7 He shall not fear an evil report;
his heart is steadfast, trusting in the LORD.
* 8 His heart is steady, he shall not fear,
until he gaze upon his adversaries.

* 9 He hath scattered abroad, he hath given to the needy; †
his justice abideth forever;
his horn shall be exalted in glory.

* 10 The wicked shall see and be vexed; †
he shall gnash his teeth and melt away.
The desire of the wicked shall perish.

Psalm 113 (112)

Lau•ate, pueri

The Lord's exaltation and condescension (cf. Isaiah 57:15)

* 1 Alleluia. †
Praise, O ye servants of the LORD,
praise the name of the LORD.
* 2 May the name of the LORD be blessed
from this time forth and forevermore.
* 3 From the rising of the sun to its setting,
the name of the LORD is to be praised.

* 4 The LORD is high above all nations;
His glory is above the heavens.
* 5 Who is like the LORD our God,
Who dwelleth on high,
* 6 Who lowereth Himself to look
upon the heavens and upon the earth?

* 7 He raiseth up the weak from the dust,
He lifteth up the needy from the dunghill,
* 8 to set him with princes,
with the princes of His people.
* 9 He maketh the barren woman to dwell in a house, †
the joyful mother of children.
Alleluia.

Psalm 114 (113A)

In exitu Israel

The wonders of the Exodus

* 1 When Israel came out of Egypt,
the house of Jacob from a barbarian people,
* 2 Judah became His sanctuary,
Israel His dominion.

* 3 The sea saw and fled;
the Jordan turned back.
* 4 The mountains skipped like rams,
the hills like lambs of the flock.

* 5 What ailed thee, O sea, that thou shouldst flee?
O Jordan, that thou shouldst turn back?
* 6 Ye mountains, that ye should skip like rams?
Ye hills, like lambs of the flock?

* 7 Before the face of the LORD, †
tremble, O earth,
before the face of the God of Jacob,
* 8 Who turned the rock into a pool of water,
the flint into a spring of water.

Psalm 115 (113B)

Non nobis Domine

The glory of the Lord and the vanity of idols

* 1 Not to us, O LORD, not to us, †
but to Thy name give glory,
for the sake of Thy mercy and Thy truth.
* 2 Why should the Gentiles say,
"Where is their God?"

* 3 But our God is in heaven;
whatsoever He willed, He hath done.
* 4 Their idols are silver and gold,
the work of men's hands.

* 5 They have a mouth, but speak not;
they have eyes, but see not.
* 6 They have ears, but hear not;
they have nostrils, but smell not.
* 7 They have hands, but feel not; †
they have feet, but walk not;
they make no sound in their throat.
* 8 Those that make them become like them;
so do all that trust in them.

* 9 O house of Israel, trust in the LORD;
He is their help and their shield.
* 10 O house of Aaron, trust in the LORD;
He is their help and their shield.
* 11 Ye that fear the LORD, trust in the LORD;
He is their help and their shield.

* 12 The LORD hath been mindful of us;
He will bless:
* He will bless the house of Israel;
He will bless the house of Aaron.
* 13 He will bless those that fear the LORD,
the little with the great.

* [14] May the LORD add to you,
to you and to your children.

* [15] May you be blessed by the LORD,
Who made heaven and earth.
* [16] The heavens are the LORD's heavens,
but the earth He hath given to the children of men.

* [17] The dead shall not praise the LORD,
nor any that go down into silence.
* [18] But we will bless the LORD
henceforth and forever. Alleluia.

Psalm 116 (114:1-9; 115)

Dilexi, quoniam exau• iet

"Love is strong as death" (Canticle of Canticles 8: 6b)

* [1] I love the LORD, because He heard
the voice of my supplications;
* [2] because He inclined His ear to me,
when in my days I would call.

* [3] The cords of death encompassed me; †
the straits of hell found me.
I found tribulation and sorrow.
* [4] Then I called upon the name of the LORD: †
"O LORD, I beseech Thee,
deliver my soul."

* [5] Gracious is the LORD and just,
and our God is compassionate.
* [6] The LORD keepeth the simple:
I was brought low, and He saved me.

* [7] Return, O my soul, to thy rest,
for the LORD hath dealt bountifully with thee.

* [8] For He hath delivered my soul from death, †
my eyes from tears,
my feet from stumbling.

* [9] I will walk before the LORD
in the land of the living.

* [10] I believed, therefore I spoke:
"I have been humbled exceedingly."
* [11] I said in my duress:
"Every man is a liar."

* [12] What shall I render to the LORD
for all His bounty to me?
* [13] I will take up the cup of salvation,
and I will call upon the name of the LORD.

* [14] I will pay my vows to the LORD
in the presence of all His people.
* [15] Precious in the sight of the LORD
is the death of His saints.

* [16] O LORD, I am Thy servant; †
I am Thy servant, the son of Thy handmaid.
Thou hast loosed my bonds.
* [17] I will sacrifice to Thee the thank-offering,
and I will call upon the name of the LORD.

* [18] I will pay my vows to the LORD,
in the presence of all His people,
* [19] in the courts of the house of the LORD, †
in thy midst, O Jerusalem.
Alleluia.

Psalm 117 (116)

Lau•ate Dominum

“Rejoice, ye Gentiles, with His people” (Romans 15:10)

* 1 O praise the LORD, all ye nations;
laud Him all ye peoples:

* 2 For strong is His mercy upon us, †
and the truth of the LORD is everlasting.
Alleluia.

Psalm 118 (117)

Confitemini Domino

“I shall not die, but live”

* 1 O give thanks to the LORD, for He is good,
for His mercy is everlasting.

* 2 Let Israel now say:
“His mercy is everlasting.”
* 3 Let the house of Aaron now say:
“His mercy is everlasting.”
* 4 Let those that fear the LORD now say:
“His mercy is everlasting.”

* 5 Out of my straits I called upon the LORD,
and the LORD answered me in a broad place.
* 6 The LORD is for me; I shall not fear.
What can man do to me?
* 7 The LORD is for me as my helper,
and I shall gaze on those that hate me.

* 8 It is better to take refuge in the LORD
than to trust in man.
* 9 It is better to take refuge in the LORD
than to trust in princes.

* [10] All nations encompassed me;
in the name of the LORD, I cut them off.
* [11] They encompassed me, encompassed me about;
in the name of the LORD, I cut them off.
* [12] They surrounded me like bees, †
and they blazed like a fire among thorns;
in the name of the LORD, I cut them off.

* [13] I was pushed hard, to the point of falling,
but the LORD helped me.
* [14] The LORD is my strength and my song,
and He hath become my salvation.
* [15] The voice of joyful cries and of salvation
is in the tents of the just.

* The right hand of the LORD hath done valiantly. †
[16] The right hand of the LORD is exalted.
The right hand of the LORD hath done valiantly.
* [17] I shall not die, but live,
and declare the works of the LORD.
* [18] The LORD hath disciplined me sorely,
but He hath not given me over to death.

* [19] Open to me the gates of justice;
I will enter through them and give thanks to the LORD.
* [20] This is the gate of the LORD;
the just shall enter through it.
* [21] I will give thanks to Thee, because Thou hast answered me
and hast become my salvation.

* [22] The stone which the builders rejected
hath become the head of the corner.
* [23] This was from the LORD;
it is marvelous in our eyes.
* [24] This is the day which the LORD hath made;
let us exult and be glad in it.

* [25] O LORD, we beseech Thee, save;
O LORD, we beseech Thee, give success.

* 26 Blessed is he who cometh †
in the name of the LORD.
We bless you from the house of the LORD.
* 27 The LORD is God,
and for us He hath made light shine.

* Begin the festal procession with boughs,
up to the horns of the altar.
* 28 Thou art my God, and I will give thanks to Thee;
my God, I will exalt Thee.

* 29 O give thanks to the LORD, for He is good,
for His mercy is everlasting.

Psalm 119 (118)

Beati Immaculati

"Father... not my will, but Thine be done" (Luke 22:42)

א Aleph

* 1 Blessed are the blameless in the way,
who walk in the law of the LORD.
* 2 Blessed are they that observe His testimonies,
that seek Him with their whole heart;
* 3 who also have done no injustice:
they have walked in His ways.
* 4 Thou hast commanded Thy precepts
to be kept diligently.
* 5 O that my ways were established
to keep Thy statutes!
* 6 Then shall I not be ashamed,
when I look to all Thy commandments.
* 7 I will confess to Thee with an upright heart,
as I learn the judgments of Thy justice.
* 8 I will keep Thy statutes;
O forsake me not utterly!

ב Beth

* 9 By what shall a youth make his path pure?
By keeping it according to Thy word.
* 10 With my whole heart have I sought Thee;
let me not err from Thy commandments.
* 11 I have hidden Thy word in my heart,
that I might not sin against Thee.
* 12 Blessed art Thou, O LORD;
teach me Thy statutes.
* 13 With my lips I have recounted
all the judgments of Thy mouth.
* 14 I rejoice in the way of Thy testimonies
as in all riches.
* 15 I will meditate on Thy precepts,
and look to Thy paths.
* 16 I will take delight in Thy statutes;
I will not forget Thy word.

ג Gimel

* 17 Deal bountifully with Thy servant, that I may live
and keep Thy word.
* 18 Unveil my eyes, that I may behold
wondrous things out of Thy law.
* 19 I am a stranger on the earth;
hide not Thy commandments from me.
* 20 My soul is consumed with longing
for Thy judgments at all times.
* 21 Thou hast rebuked the insolent, the accursèd,
who err from Thy commandments.
* 22 Remove from me reproach and contempt,
for I have observed Thy testimonies.
* 23 Although princes have sat talking against me,
Thy servant will meditate on Thy statutes.
* 24 Indeed Thy testimonies are my delight,
the men of my counsel.

ד Daleth

* 25 My soul cleaveth to the dust;
  quicken me according to Thy word.
* 26 I declared my ways, and Thou didst answer me;
  teach me Thy statutes.
* 27 Make me understand the way of Thy precepts,
  and I will meditate on Thy wonders.
* 28 My soul melteth for sorrow;
  raise me up according to Thy word.
* 29 Remove from me the way of falsehood,
  and grace me with Thy law.
* 30 I have chosen the way of faithfulness;
  I have set Thy judgments before me.
* 31 I have stuck to Thy testimonies;
  O LORD, put me not to shame.
* 32 I will run the way of Thy commandments
  when Thou shalt widen my heart.

ה He

* 33 Teach me, O LORD, the way of Thy statutes,
  and I will observe it to the end.
* 34 Give me understanding, and I will observe Thy law
  and keep it with my whole heart.
* 35 Lead me in the path of Thy commandments,
  for this have I desired.
* 36 Incline my heart unto Thy testimonies,
  and not unto gain.
* 37 Turn away my eyes from looking at vanity;
  quicken me in Thy way.
* 38 Confirm Thy word to Thy servant,
  that Thou mayest be feared.
* 39 Turn away my reproach, which I dread,
  for Thy judgments are good.
* 40 Behold, I have longed for Thy precepts;
  quicken me in Thy justice.

ו Waw

* [41] Let Thy mercy also come to me, O LORD,
Thy salvation according to Thy word.
* [42] And I shall answer with a word those who reproach me,
for I trust in Thy word.
* [43] And take not the word of truth utterly out of my mouth,
for I have hoped in Thy judgments.
* [44] So I will keep Thy law continually,
forever and ever.
* [45] And I will walk in a roomy place,
for I have sought Thy precepts.
* [46] I will also speak of Thy testimonies before kings,
and will not be ashamed.
* [47] And I will take delight in Thy commandments,
which I have loved.
* [48] And I will lift up my hands to Thy commandments,
which I have loved,
and I will meditate on Thy statutes.

ז Zayin

* [49] Remember Thy word to Thy servant,
in which Thou hast made me hope.
* [50] This is my comfort in my affliction,
that Thy word hath quickened me.
* [51] The insolent have utterly scoffed at me,
but I have not declined from Thy law.
* [52] I have remembered Thy judgments from of old, O LORD,
and I have taken comfort.
* [53] Indignation hath seized me because of the wicked,
that forsake Thy law.
* [54] Thy statutes have been my psalms
in the house of my pilgrimage.
* [55] I have remembered Thy name in the night, O LORD,
and I have kept Thy law.
* [56] This hath been mine,
that I have observed Thy precepts.

ח Heth

* [57] My portion, O LORD, I have said,
  is to keep Thy words.
* [58] I have entreated Thy face with all my heart;
  be gracious to me according to Thy word.
* [59] I considered my ways,
  and turned my feet to Thy testimonies.
* [60] I made haste and did not delay
  to keep Thy commandments.
* [61] The cords of the wicked encircled me,
  but I forgot not Thy law.
* [62] At midnight I rise to confess to Thee,
  because of the judgments of Thy justice.
* [63] I am a companion of all that fear Thee,
  and that keep Thy precepts.
* [64] The earth, O LORD, is full of Thy mercy:
  Teach me Thy statutes.

ט Teth

* [65] Thou hast dealt well with Thy servant,
  O LORD, according to Thy word.
* [66] Teach me good discernment and knowledge,
  for I have believed in Thy commandments.
* [67] Before I was humbled, I erred,
  but now I keep Thy word.
* [68] Thou art good and doest good;
  teach me Thy statutes.
* [69] The arrogant have smeared me with falsehood,
  but with all my heart I will keep Thy precepts.
* [70] Their heart is gross like fat,
  but I take delight in Thy law.
* [71] It is good for me that I have been humbled,
  that I might learn Thy statutes.
* [72] Better to me is the law of Thy mouth
  than thousands of gold and silver.

י Yodh

* [73] Thy hands have made me and established me;
give me understanding, and I will learn Thy commandments.
* [74] Those that fear Thee shall see me and rejoice,
because I have hoped in Thy word.
* [75] I know, O LORD, that Thy judgments are just,
and that in faithfulness Thou hast humbled me.
* [76] Let Thy mercy be for my comfort
according to Thy word to Thy servant.
* [77] Let Thy compassion come to me, and I shall live,
for Thy law is my delight.
* [78] Let the insolent be shamed, for they diverted me
with falsehood;
but I will meditate on Thy precepts.
* [79] Let those that fear Thee turn to me,
and those that know Thy testimonies.
* [80] Let my heart be blameless in Thy statutes,
that I may not be ashamed.

כ Kaph

* [81] My soul hath fainted for Thy salvation;
in Thy word have I hoped.
* [82] My eyes have failed for Thy word,
saying, "When wilt Thou comfort me?"
* [83] Though I have become like a wineskin in the smoke,
I have not forgotten Thy statutes.
* [84] How many are the days of Thy servant?
When wilt Thou do judgment against those
that persecute me?
* [85] The arrogant have dug pits for me,
which is not according to Thy law.
* [86] All Thy commandments are faithful;
they have persecuted me with falsehood; help me!
* [87] They had almost made an end of me on earth,
but I forsook not Thy precepts.
* [88] Quicken me according to Thy mercy,
and I will keep the testimonies of Thy mouth.

ל Lamedh

* [89] Forever, O LORD, Thy word
standeth fast in the heavens.
* [90] From generation to generation is Thy faithfulness;
Thou hast established the earth, and it standeth.
* [91] According to Thy judgments, they have stood to this day,
for all things are Thy servants.
* [92] If Thy law had not been my delight,
then I would have perished in my humiliation.
* [93] I will never forget Thy precepts,
for by them Thou hast given me life.
* [94] I am Thine; save me,
for I have sought Thy precepts.
* [95] The wicked have waited for me to destroy me,
but I give heed to Thy testimonies.
* [96] I have seen a limit to all perfection,
but Thy commandment is exceedingly broad.

מ Mem

* [97] O how I have loved Thy law!
It is my meditation all the day.
* [98] Thy commandment maketh me wiser than my enemies,
for it is ever with me.
* [99] I have more insight than all my teachers,
because Thy testimonies are my meditation.
* [100] I have understood more than the agèd,
because I have observed Thy precepts.
* [101] I have withheld my feet from every evil path,
in order to keep Thy word.
* [102] I have not turned aside from Thy judgments,
because Thou hast taught me.
* [103] How sweet are Thy words to my palate,
more than honey to my mouth!
* [104] From Thy precepts I get understanding;
therefore I hate every false path.

נ Nun

* [105] Thy word is a lamp unto my feet
and a light unto my path.
* [106] I have sworn and have confirmed it,
to keep the judgments of Thy justice.
* [107] I have been humbled exceedingly, O LORD;
quicken me according to Thy word.
* [108] Be pleased with the freewill offerings of my
mouth, O LORD,
and teach me Thy judgments.
* [109] My soul is continually in my hand,
yet I have not forgotten Thy law.
* [110] The wicked have laid a snare for me,
but I have not strayed from Thy precepts.
* [111] Thy testimonies are my inheritance forever,
for they are the joy of my heart.
* [112] I have inclined my heart to do Thy statutes
forever, unto the end.

ס Samekh

* [113] I have hated the half-hearted,
and I have loved Thy law.
* [114] Thou art my hiding place and my shield;
I have hoped in Thy word.
* [115] Depart from me, ye evildoers,
and I will observe the commandments of my God.
* [116] Uphold me according to Thy word, and I shall live,
and confound me not in my expectation.
* [117] Sustain me, and I shall be saved
and have regard for Thy statutes continually.
* [118] Thou hast spurned all that err from Thy statutes,
for their deceit is falsehood.
* [119] All the wicked of the earth Thou hast removed like dross;
therefore have I loved Thy testimonies.
* [120] My flesh shuddereth from dread of Thee,
and I am afraid of Thy judgments.

ע Ayin

* 121 I have done judgment and justice;
leave me not to my oppressors.
* 122 Be surety for Thy servant for good;
let not the arrogant oppress me.
* 123 My eyes have failed for Thy salvation,
and for the word of Thy justice.
* 124 Deal with Thy servant according to Thy mercy,
and teach me Thy statutes.
* 125 I am Thy servant; give me understanding,
that I may know Thy testimonies.
* 126 It is time for the LORD to act:
they have broken Thy law.
* 127 Therefore I love Thy commandments
above gold and above fine gold.
* 128 Therefore I direct myself by all Thy precepts;
I hate every false path.

פ Pe

* 129 Thy testimonies are wonderful;
therefore my soul hath observed them.
* 130 The disclosure of Thy words sheddeth light,
giving understanding to the simple.
* 131 I opened my mouth and I panted,
because I longed for Thy commandments.
* 132 Turn to me and be gracious to me,
according to Thy judgment for those that love Thy name.
* 133 Establish my steps according to Thy word,
and let no wrong get dominion over me.
* 134 Redeem me from the oppression of man,
that I may keep Thy precepts.
* 135 Make Thy face to shine upon Thy servant,
and teach me Thy statutes.
* 136 Streams of water have run down my eyes,
because they have not kept Thy law.

צ Sadhe

* 137 Just art Thou, O LORD,
and right are Thy judgments.
* 138 Thou hast commanded Thy testimonies in justice
and in exceeding faithfulness.
* 139 My zeal hath consumed me,
because my adversaries have forgotten Thy words.
* 140 Thy word is exceedingly refined,
and Thy servant hath loved it.
* 141 I am little and despised,
yet I have not forgotten Thy precepts.
* 142 Thy justice is justice forever,
and Thy law is truth.
* 143 Tribulation and straits have found me,
yet Thy commandments are my delight.
* 144 Thy testimonies are justice forever;
give me understanding, and I shall live.

ק Qoph

* 145 I have called with my whole heart, answer me, O LORD;
I will observe Thy statutes.
* 146 I have called to Thee, save me,
and I will keep Thy testimonies.
* 147 I preceded the morning twilight and cried for help;
I hoped in Thy words.
* 148 My eyes preceded the watches of the night,
that I might meditate on Thy words.
* 149 Hear my voice according to Thy mercy, O LORD;
quicken me according to Thy judgment.
* 150 Those that persecute me with cunning have drawn near;
they are far from Thy law.
* 151 Thou art near, O LORD,
and all Thy commandments are truth.
* 152 From of old have I known of Thy testimonies
that Thou hast founded them forever.

ר Resh

* 153 See my humiliation and deliver me,
for I have not forgotten Thy law.
* 154 Plead my cause and redeem me;
quicken me for the sake of Thy word.
* 155 Salvation is far from the wicked,
because they have not sought Thy statutes.
* 156 Thy compassions are many, O LORD;
quicken me according to Thy judgment.
* 157 Many are my persecutors and adversaries,
yet I have not declined from Thy testimonies.
* 158 I looked at the faithless with loathing,
because they did not keep Thy words.
* 159 See that I have loved Thy precepts;
O LORD, quicken me according to Thy mercy.
* 160 The sum of Thy word is truth;
and all the judgments of Thy justice are forever.

ש Sin/Shin

* 161 Princes have persecuted me without cause,
but my heart trembleth at Thy words.
* 162 I rejoice at Thy word
as one that findeth much spoil.
* 163 Falsehood I have hated and abhorred,
but Thy law I have loved.
* 164 Seven times a day I have praised Thee,
for the judgments of Thy justice.
* 165 Much peace have they that love Thy law,
and there is no stumbling block for them.
* 166 I have expected Thy salvation, O LORD,
and I have done Thy commandments.
* 167 My soul hath kept Thy testimonies,
and I have loved them exceedingly.
* 168 I have kept Thy precepts and Thy testimonies,
for all my ways are before Thee.

ת Taw

* 169 Let my cry come before Thee, O LORD;
  give me understanding according to Thy word.
* 170 Let my supplication come before Thee;
  deliver me according to Thy word.
* 171 My lips shall pour forth praise,
  when Thou shalt teach me Thy statutes.
* 172 My tongue shall sing Thy word,
  for all Thy commandments are just.
* 173 Let Thy hand be to help me,
  since I have chosen Thy precepts.
* 174 I have longed for Thy salvation, O LORD,
  and Thy law is my delight.
* 175 Let my soul live and praise Thee,
  and let Thy judgments help me.
* 176 I have gone astray like a lost sheep; seek Thy servant,
  for I have not forgotten Thy commandments.

Psalm 120 (119)

Ad Dominum

Starting the Ascents: I sojourn far from the sanctuary

1 *A Song of Ascents.*

* In my distress I called to the LORD,
and He answered me.
* 2 O LORD, deliver my soul from lying lips,
from a deceitful tongue.

* 3 What shall be given to thee and what added to thee,
O deceitful tongue?
* 4 The sharpened arrows of the mighty,
with coals of the broom tree.

* 5 Woe is me, that I sojourn in Mesech,
that I dwell among the tents of Kedar.

* 6 Too long hath my soul dwelt
with those that hate peace.
* 7 I am peaceable, but when I speak,
they are for battle.

Psalm 121 (120)

Levavi oculos

"His parents went [up] yearly to Jerusalem for Passover"

(Luke 2: 41, 42)

1 *A Song of Ascents.*

* I will lift up my eyes to the mountains;
from whence shall my help come?
* 2 My help is from the LORD,
Who made heaven and earth.

* 3 He will not suffer thy foot to be moved;
He that keepeth thee will not slumber.
* 4 Behold, He shall neither slumber nor sleep
that keepeth Israel.

* 5 The LORD is thy keeper; †
the LORD is thy shade
at thy right hand.
* 6 By day the sun shall not smite thee,
nor the moon by night.

* 7 The LORD will keep thee from all evil;
He will keep thy soul.
* 8 The LORD will keep thy going out and thy coming in
from this time forth and forevermore.

Psalm 122 (121)

Laetatus sum in his

Jerusalem, city of unity, judgment, and peace

1 *A Song of Ascents. Of David.*

* I rejoiced when they said to me:
"Let us go to the house of the LORD."
* 2 Our feet have been standing
within thy gates, O Jerusalem.

* 3 Jerusalem is built as a city
that is joined to itself together.
* 4 Thither the tribes went up,
the tribes of the LORD,
* as a testimony to Israel,
to give thanks to the name of the LORD.
* 5 For there were set thrones for judgment,
the thrones of the house of David.

* 6 Pray for the peace of Jerusalem:
"May they be secure that love thee.
* 7 May peace be within thy ramparts,
and security in thy fortified palaces."

* 8 For the sake of my brethren and my friends,
I will say, "Peace be within thee."
* 9 For the sake of the house of the LORD our God,
I will seek thy good.

Psalm 123 (122)

A• te levavi

"To the humble, He gives grace"
(Proverbs 3:34; James 4:6; 1 Peter 5:5)

1 *A Song of Ascents.*

* To Thee have I lifted up my eyes,
O Thou Who dwellest in the heavens.

* 2 Behold, as the eyes of servants
are on the hand of their masters,
* as the eyes of a handmaid
are on the hand of her mistress,
* so our eyes are on the LORD our God,
till He be gracious to us.

* 3 Be gracious to us, O LORD, be gracious to us,
for we are more than sated with contempt.
* 4 Our soul is more than sated †
with the mockery of those that are at ease,
with the contempt of the proud.

Psalm 124 (123)

Nisi quia Dominus

The maker of all is our help

1 *A Song of Ascents. Of David.*

* Had it not been the LORD Who was for us —
let Israel now say —
* 2 had it not been the LORD Who was for us,
when men rose up against us,
* 3 then would they have swallowed us up alive,
when their anger was kindled against us.
* 4 Then the waters would have swept over us,
the torrent would have passed over our soul;
* 5 then over our soul would have passed
the raging waters.

* 6 Blessed be the LORD,
Who did not give us a prey to their teeth.
* 7 Our soul hath escaped like a bird
from the snare of the fowlers.
* The snare was broken,
and we escaped.

* 8 Our help is in the name of the LORD,
Who made heaven and earth.

Psalm 125 (124)

Qui confi• unt

A righteous nation will not remain subject to evil rulers

1 *A Song of Ascents.*

* Those that trust in the LORD are like Mount Zion,
which cannot be moved, but abideth forever.

* 2 As the mountains are round about Jerusalem, †
so the LORD is round about His people
from this time forth and forevermore.

* 3 For the scepter of wickedness shall not rest
upon the lot of the just,
* lest the just stretch forth their hands
to act unrighteously.

* 4 Do good, O LORD, to the good,
and to those that are upright in their hearts.
* 5 But those that turn aside their crooked ways, †
the LORD will lead away with the wrongdoers.
Peace be upon Israel.

Psalm 126 (125)

In converten•o

"Sow here in tears, but there [eternity] reap in joy"
(St. Elizabeth Ann Seton)

1 *A Song of Ascents.*

* When the LORD restored the fortunes of Zion,
we were like them that dream.
* 2 Then was our mouth filled with laughter,
and our tongue with shouts of joy.

* Then they said among the nations:
"The LORD hath done great things with them."
* 3 The LORD hath done great things with us;
we were glad.

* 4 Restore our fortunes, O LORD,
as the watercourses in the Southland.
* 5 They that sow in tears
shall reap with shouts of joy.

* 6 He that went forth weeping,
carrying the seed for sowing,
* shall come back with shouts of joy,
carrying his sheaves.

Psalm 127 (126)

Nisi Dominus

"Without me you can do nothing" (John 15:5)

1 *A Song of Ascents. Of Solomon.*

* Unless the LORD build the house,
its builders will have laboured in vain.
* Unless the LORD keep the city,
its keeper will have watched in vain.

* 2 It is vain for you to rise up early
and to go late to rest,
* you that eat the bread of toil;
for He giveth to His beloved sleep.

* 3 Lo, children are a heritage from the LORD,
the fruit of the womb is a reward.
* 4 As arrows in the hand of a warrior,
so are the children of one's youth.

* 5 Blessed is the man
who hath filled his quiver with them.
* He shall not be ashamed,
when he shall speak with his enemies in the gate.

Psalm 128 (127)

Beati omnes

The domestic church

1 *A Song of Ascents.*

* Blessed is everyone who feareth the LORD,
who walketh in His ways.

* 2 Thou shalt eat the labour of thy hands;
blessed art thou, and it shall be well with thee.
* 3 Thy wife shall be like a fruitful vine
in the recesses of thy house;
* thy children like olive shoots
around thy table.

* 4 Behold, thus shall the man be blessed
who feareth the LORD.
* 5 May the LORD bless thee from Zion, †
and mayest thou see the good of Jerusalem
all the days of thy life,
* 6 and mayest thou see thy children's children.
Peace be upon Israel.

Psalm 129 (128)

Saepe expugnaverunt

Against the enemies of the Church

[1] *A Song of Ascents.*

* Much have they assailed me from my youth —
let Israel now say —
* [2] much have they assailed me from my youth,
but they have not prevailed against me.

* [3] The plowmen plowed upon my back;
they made long their furrows.
* [4] The LORD is just;
He hath cut the cords of the wicked.

* [5] Let them be shamed and turned back,
all that hate Zion.
* [6] Let them be as grass upon the housetops,
which withereth before it springeth up:

* [7] Wherewith the reaper filleth not his hand,
nor the gatherer of sheaves his bosom;
* [8] and those that pass by do not say, †
"The blessing of the LORD be unto you;
we bless you in the name of the LORD."

Psalm 130 (129)

De profun• is

Daily monastic prayer for the dead

(Sixth Penitential Psalm)

[1] *A Song of Ascents.*

* Out of the depths have I cried to Thee, O LORD;
[2] Lord, hear my voice.
* Let Thy ears be attentive
to the voice of my supplications.

* [3] If Thou, O LORD, wilt mark iniquities,
Lord, who shall stand?
* [4] But with Thee is forgiveness,
that Thou mayest be feared.

* [5] I have waited for the LORD, †
my soul hath waited,
and in His word I have hoped.
* [6] My soul hath waited for the LORD
from the morning watch even until night.
* From the morning watch,
[7] let Israel hope in the LORD.

* Because with the LORD there is mercy,
and with Him is plenteous redemption.
* [8] And He will redeem Israel
from all his iniquities.

Psalm 131 (130)

Domine, non est

The prayer of quiet

(cf. St. Teresa of Avila, *Interior Castle,* Fourth Mansions, Ch. 2)

1 *A Song of Ascents. Of Davi•.*

* O LORD, my heart is not exalted,
nor are my eyes lifted up.
* Neither have I walked in great things,
nor in things too marvelous for me.

* 2 But I have settled and stilled my soul,
as a nursed child with his mother;
* as a nursed child,
so is my soul within me.

* 3 O Israel, hope in the LORD
from this time forth and forevermore.

Psalm 132 (131)

Memento, Domine

The election of David and of Zion

1 *A Song of Ascents.*

* Remember, O LORD, to David's merit,
all his meekness;
* 2 that he swore to the LORD,
made a vow to the Mighty One of Jacob:

* 3 "I will not enter the tent of my house;
I will not go up onto the couch of my bed;
* 4 I will not give sleep to my eyes,
to my eyelids any slumber,

* [5] until I find a place for the LORD,
a tabernacle for the Mighty One of Jacob."

* [6] Lo, we heard of it in Ephratha;
we found it in the fields of Jaar.
* [7] Let us enter into His tabernacle;
let us worship at His footstool.

* [8] Arise, O LORD, unto Thy resting place,
Thou and the ark of Thy strength.
* [9] Let Thy priests be clothed with justice,
and Thy saints ring out their joy.
* [10] For Thy servant David's sake,
turn not away the face of Thy anointed.

* [11] The LORD swore the truth to David,
and He will not turn back from it:
* "Of the fruit of thy womb
will I set upon thy throne.
* [12] If thy sons will keep My covenant
and My testimonies which I shall teach them,
* their sons also forever
shall sit upon thy throne."

* [13] For the LORD hath chosen Zion;
He hath desired it for His habitation.
* [14] "This is My resting place forever;
here will I dwell, for I have desired it.

* [15] I will abundantly bless her provisions;
her needy I will satisfy with bread.
* [16] Her priests I will clothe with salvation,
and her saints shall ring out merrily their joy.

* [17] There will I make a horn to sprout for David;
I have prepared a lamp for My anointed.
* [18] His enemies I will clothe with shame,
but upon himself shall his diadem flourish."

Psalm 133 (132)

Ecce quam bonum

The communion of saints

1 *A Song of Ascents. Of David.*

* Behold how good and how pleasant it is
for brethren to dwell together in unity.

* 2 It is like the good oil upon the head, †
coming down upon the beard, the beard of Aaron,
coming down upon the neck of his garments.

* 3 It is like the dew of Hermon coming down
upon the mountains of Zion;
* for there the LORD commanded the blessing,
life forevermore.

Psalm 134 (133)

Ecce nunc benedicite

Concluding the Ascents: "Compline" near the sanctuary

1 *A Song of Ascents.*

* Behold, bless ye the LORD, †
all ye servants of the LORD,
who stand by night in the house of the LORD.

* 2 Lift up your hands to the sanctuary,
and bless ye the LORD.

* 3 May the LORD bless thee out of Zion,
He Who made heaven and earth.

Psalm 135 (134)

Lau•ate nomen

"He will be comforted regarding His servants"

(2 Maccabees 7:6; cf. v14b and Deuteronomy 23:36, Greek)

* 1 Alleluia. †
Praise ye the name of the LORD,
praise, O ye servants of the LORD,
* 2 that stand in the house of the LORD,
in the courts of the house of our God.

* 3 Praise the LORD, for the LORD is good;
sing a psalm to His name, for it is sweet.
* 4 For the LORD hath chosen Jacob for Himself,
Israel for His own possession.

* 5 For I know that the LORD is great,
and that our Lord is above all gods.
* 6 Whatsoever the LORD willed, He hath done, †
in heaven and on earth,
in the seas and in all deeps.
* 7 Bringing up clouds from the end of the earth, †
He maketh lightning for the rain;
He bringeth forth the wind from His storehouses.

* 8 He it was Who smote the firstborn of Egypt,
from man even unto beast.
* 9 He sent forth signs and portents †
in the midst of thee, O Egypt,
upon Pharaoh and upon all his servants;

* 10 Who smote many nations
and slew strong kings:
* 11 Sihon, king of the Amorites, †
and Og, king of Bashan,
and all the kingdoms of Canaan.

* 12 And He gave their land as an inheritance,
an inheritance to Israel His people.

* 13 O LORD, Thy name is everlasting;
O LORD, Thy memorial is from generation to generation.
* 14 For the LORD will judge His people
and have compassion on His servants.

* 15 The idols of the Gentiles are silver and gold,
the work of men's hands.
* 16 They have a mouth, but they speak not;
they have eyes, but they see not.
* 17 They have ears, but they hear not,
nor is there any breath in their mouth.
* 18 Those that make them shall be like them,
and all that trust in them.

* 19 O house of Israel, bless the LORD;
O house of Aaron, bless the LORD;
* 20 O house of Levi, bless the LORD;
you that fear the LORD, bless the LORD.

* 21 Blessed be the LORD out of Zion,
He Who dwelleth in Jerusalem. Alleluia.

Psalm 136 (135)

Confitemini Domino

The everlasting mercy: the Great Hallel

(cf. Pope Benedict XVI, General Audience of 19 October 2011)

* 1 O give thanks to the LORD, for He is good,
for His mercy is everlasting.
* 2 Give thanks to the God of gods,
for His mercy is everlasting.
* 3 Give thanks to the Lord of lords,
for His mercy is everlasting.

* 4 To Him Who alone doth great wonders,
for His mercy is everlasting;
* 5 to Him Who made the heavens in understanding,
for His mercy is everlasting;
* 6 to Him Who spread firm the earth above the waters,
for His mercy is everlasting;
* 7 to Him Who made the great lights,
for His mercy is everlasting;
* 8 the sun to rule over the day,
for His mercy is everlasting;
* 9 the moon and stars to rule over the night,
for His mercy is everlasting.

* 10 To Him Who smote Egypt in their firstborn,
for His mercy is everlasting;
* 11 and brought out Israel from among them,
for His mercy is everlasting;
* 12 with a strong hand and an outstretched arm,
for His mercy is everlasting.

* 13 To Him Who divided the Red Sea into parts,
for His mercy is everlasting;
* 14 and made Israel pass through the midst of it,
for His mercy is everlasting;

* [15] and shook off Pharaoh and his force into the Red Sea,
for His mercy is everlasting.

* [16] To Him Who led His people through the wilderness,
for His mercy is everlasting;
* [17] to Him Who smote great kings,
for His mercy is everlasting;
* [18] and slew magnificent kings,
for His mercy is everlasting;
* [19] Sihon, king of the Amorites,
for His mercy is everlasting;
* [20] and Og, king of Bashan,
for His mercy is everlasting;
* [21] and He gave their land as an inheritance,
for His mercy is everlasting;
* [22] an inheritance to Israel His servant,
for His mercy is everlasting.

* [23] Who remembered us in our humiliation,
for His mercy is everlasting;
* [24] and snatched us from our adversaries,
for His mercy is everlasting;
* [25] Who giveth food to all flesh,
for His mercy is everlasting.

* [26] O give thanks to the God of heaven,
for His mercy is everlasting.

Psalm 137 (136)

Super flumina Babylonis

"To dash at once against Christ [infant] evil thoughts"

(cf. Rule of St. Benedict, Prologue 28 and 4:50)

* 1 By the rivers of Babylon, †
there we sat down and wept,
as we remembered Zion.
* 2 On the willows in the midst of it
we hung up our harps.

* 3 For there they that led us captive †
asked of us words of song,
and our tormentors mirth:
* "Sing to us
one of the songs of Zion."

* 4 How shall we sing †
the song of the LORD
in a foreign land?
* 5 If I forget thee, O Jerusalem,
let my right hand forget her cunning.

* 6 Let my tongue cleave †
to the roof of my mouth,
if I remember thee not,
* if I exalt not Jerusalem
above my utmost joy.

* 7 Remember, O LORD, †
against the children of Edom,
the day of Jerusalem,
* who said, "Raze it!
Raze it to its foundation!"

* 8 O daughter of Babylon, waster, †
blessed is he who shall repay to thee thy requital,
which thou hast requited to us.
* 9 Blessed is he who shall lay hold of and dash
thy little ones against the rock.

Psalm 138 (137)

Confitebor tibi

Liturgy in the presence of the angels

(cf. Rule of St Benedict, 19:5-6)

1 *Of David.*

* I will confess to Thee, O LORD, with my whole heart.
In the sight of the angels I will sing psalms to Thee.
* 2 I will adore toward Thy holy temple †
and confess Thy name
for Thy mercy and Thy truth.

* For Thou hast magnified above all
Thy name and Thy word.
* 3 On the day I called, Thou didst answer me;
Thou didst multiply strength in my soul.

* 4 All the kings of the earth shall confess to Thee, O LORD,
when they have heard the words of Thy mouth.
* 5 And they shall sing of the ways of the LORD,
for great is the glory of the LORD.

* 6 For the LORD is high, yet He looketh on the lowly,
and the proud He knoweth from afar.
* 7 Though I walk in the midst of trouble,
Thou wilt quicken me;
* Thou shalt stretch forth Thy hand †
against the wrath of my enemies,
and Thy right hand shall save me.

* 8 The LORD will accomplish what pertaineth to me. †
Thy mercy, O LORD, is everlasting;
abandon not the work of Thy hands.

Psalm 139 (138)

Domine, probasti

God omniscient and omnipresent

1 *To the choirmaster. A Psalm of David.*

* O LORD, Thou hast searched me and known me; †
2 Thou hast known my sitting down and my rising up;
Thou hast understood my thoughts from afar.
* 3 Thou hast searched out my path and my lying down,
and art familiar with all my ways.

* 4 For there is not yet an utterance on my tongue,
but lo, O LORD, Thou knowest it altogether.
* 5 Thou hast besieged me behind and before,
and laid Thy hand upon me.
* 6 Such knowledge is too wonderful for me;
it is high, I cannot attain it.

* 7 Whither shall I go from Thy Spirit?
Or whither shall I flee from Thy face?
* 8 If I ascend into heaven, Thou art there;
if I make my bed in hell, lo, Thou art there.
* 9 And if I take the wings of the dawn
and dwell in the uttermost parts of the sea,
* 10 even there Thy hand shall lead me,
and Thy right hand shall take hold of me.

* 11 If I say, "Surely darkness shall overwhelm me,
and the light about me be night,"
* 12 even darkness is not dark for Thee, †
and the night is as bright as the day —
for as is the darkness, so is the light.

* 13 For Thou didst create my reins;
Thou didst weave me in my mother's womb.

* [14] I thank Thee that I am fearfully, wonderfully made; †
wonderful are Thy works,
and my soul knoweth it right well.

* [15] My bones were not hidden from Thee, †
when I was being made in secret,
finely embroidered in the depths of the earth.
* [16] Thy eyes saw my formless substance,
and in Thy book they were all written —
* the days that were formed,
when as yet there was none of them.

* [17] But to me, how precious are Thy thoughts, O God;
how mighty is their sum.
* [18] Should I count them, they would be more numerous
than the sand.
Should I come to the end, I would still be with Thee.

* [19] If Thou wouldst but slay the wicked, O God,
and that men of blood might depart from me,
* [20] who speak of Thee maliciously,
who lift themselves up against Thee in vain.
* [21] Do I not hate them, O LORD, that hate Thee,
and loathe them that rise up against Thee?
* [22] With a perfect hatred have I hated them;
they have become enemies to me.

* [23] Search me, O God, and know my heart;
try me and know my cares.
* [24] And see if there be any grievous way in me,
and lead me in the way everlasting.

Psalm 140 (139)

Eripe me, Domine

"The upright shall dwell [serenely] in Thy presence"

1 *To the choirmaster. A Psalm of David.*

* 2 Deliver me, O LORD, from the evil man,
from the violent man preserve me,
* 3 who have devised evil things in their heart;
they stir up wars every day.
* 4 They have sharpened their tongue like a serpent;
the venom of asps is under their lips. *Selah*

* 5 Keep me, O LORD, from the hands of the wicked, †
from the violent man preserve me,
who have devised to trip up my steps.
* 6 The proud have hidden a snare for me, †
and spread out cords as a net;
by the wayside they have set traps for me. *Selah*

* 7 I have said to the LORD, "Thou art my God."
Give ear, O LORD, to the voice of my supplications.
* 8 O LORD, my Lord, the strength of my salvation,
Thou hast covered my head in the day of battle.
* 9 Grant not, O LORD, the desires of the wicked,
nor further his device. *Selah*

* 10 Those who surround me lift up their head;
let the mischief of their lips cover them.
* 11 Let burning coals fall upon them;
let them be cast into pits, no more to rise.
* 12 A man of the tongue shall not be established in the land;
evil shall hunt down the violent with thrust upon thrust.

* 13 I know that the LORD will take up the cause of the poor,
the judgment of the needy.
* 14 Surely the just shall give thanks to Thy name;
the upright shall dwell in Thy presence.

Psalm 141 (140)

Domine, clamavi

Evening prayer for protection

1 *A Psalm of David.*

* O LORD, I have called to Thee, hasten to me;
give ear to my voice when I call to Thee.
* 2 Let my prayer be established as incense before Thee,
the lifting up of my hands as the evening sacrifice.

* 3 Set a watch, O LORD, upon my mouth,
and a guard at the door of my lips.
* 4 Incline not my heart unto an evil word, †
to practise wicked deeds with men who are wrongdoers,
and let me not eat of their dainties.
* 5 Let the just man strike me in mercy and rebuke me; †
it is oil for the head, which my head shall not refuse;
for my prayer is continually against their evil deeds.

* 6 When their judges are thrown down beside the rock,
then they shall heed my words, for they were pleasant.
* 7 As one who is cloven and split upon the ground,
so shall their bones be scattered at the mouth of hell.

* 8 But my eyes are toward Thee, O LORD, my Lord;
in Thee have I taken refuge, pour not out my soul.
* 9 Keep me from the snare that they have laid for me,
and from the traps of the wrongdoers.
* 10 Let the wicked fall into their own nets,
while I alone pass on.

Psalm 142 (141)

Voce mea

"Bring my soul out of prison"

1 *A Maskil of David, when he was in the cave. A prayer.*

* 2 With my voice I cry to the LORD;
with my voice I make supplication to the LORD.
* 3 I pour out my meditation before Him;
I declare my trouble before Him.
* 4 When my spirit fainteth within me,
then Thou knowest my path.

* In the way wherein I walk,
they have hidden a snare for me.
* 5 I look to the right and see,
that there is none taking notice of me;
* flight hath failed me;
there is none who inquireth about my soul.

* 6 I have cried to Thee, O LORD. †
I have said, "Thou art my refuge,
my portion in the land of the living."
* 7 Attend to my outcry,
for I am brought very low.

* Deliver me from my persecutors,
for they are too steadfast for me.
* 8 Bring my soul out of prison,
that I may give thanks to Thy name.
* The just will surround me,
for Thou wilt deal bountifully with me.

Psalm 143 (142)

Domine, exau•i

"No flesh shall be justified...by works of the law" (Romans 3:20)

(Seventh Penitential Psalm)

1 *A Psalm of Davi•.*

* O LORD, hear my prayer; †
give ear to my supplications in Thy faithfulness;
answer me in Thy justice.
* 2 And enter not into judgment with Thy servant,
for no man living shall be justified in Thy sight.

* 3 For the enemy hath persecuted my soul;
he hath crushed my life to the ground.
* He hath made me dwell in darkness
as those long dead.
* 4 And so my spirit hath fainted within me;
my heart within me is appalled.

* 5 I remember the days of old; †
I meditate on all Thy deeds;
I reflect on the works of Thy hands;
* 6 I spread forth my hands to Thee;
my soul is as a parched land toward Thee. *Selah*

* 7 Make haste to answer me, O LORD;
my spirit faileth.
* Hide not Thy face from me,
lest I become like those that go down into the pit.

* 8 Make me hear Thy mercy in the morning,
for in Thee have I trusted.
* Make me know the way wherein I should walk,
for to Thee have I lifted up my soul.

* 9 Deliver me from my enemies, O LORD.
To Thee have I fled for refuge.
* 10 Teach me to do Thy will,
for Thou art my God.
* Let Thy good Spirit lead me
on level ground.

* 11 For Thy name's sake, O LORD, quicken me.
In Thy justice bring my soul out of trouble.
* 12 And in Thy mercy, put an end to my enemies, †
and make all the adversaries of my soul perish,
for I am Thy servant.

Psalm 144 (143)

Bene• ictus Dominus

Prayer for national victory and prosperity

1 *A Psalm of Davi•.*

* Blessed be the LORD, my rock, †
Who traineth my hands for battle,
and my fingers for war.
* 2 My mercy and my fortress,
my high place and my deliverer,
* my shield, and He in Whom I take refuge,
Who subdueth my people under me.

* 3 O LORD, what is man that Thou shouldst know him,
the son of man, that Thou shouldst consider him?
* 4 Man is like unto vanity,
his days are like a passing shadow.

* 5 O LORD, bow Thy heavens and come down;
touch the mountains, and they will smoke.
* 6 Flash forth lightning and scatter them;
send out Thy arrows and rout them.

* [7] Stretch out Thy hand from on high; †
release me and deliver me from many waters,
from the hand of foreigners,
* [8] whose mouths speak vanity,
and whose right hand is a right hand of falsehood.

* [9] O God, I will sing a new song to Thee;
with a psaltery of ten strings I will chant a psalm to Thee,
* [10] Who givest salvation to kings,
Who releasest David Thy servant from the evil sword.
* [11] Release me and deliver me
from the hand of foreigners,
* whose mouths speak vanity,
and whose right hand is a right hand of falsehood.

* [12] Then our sons will be as plants,
grown tall in their youth;
* our daughters will be as corner pillars,
carved for the structure of the temple.
* [13] Our storehouses will be full,
affording all manner of store.
* Our sheep will be in the thousands, †
tens of thousands in our fields;
[14] our cattle will be fat.
* There will be no breach, nor going forth,
nor outcry in our public places.

* [15] Blessed the people to whom it shall be thus;
blessed the people whose God is the LORD.

Psalm 145 (144)

Exaltabo te, Deus

The divine attributes

1 *A Song of Praise. Of Davi•.*

* I will exalt Thee, my God, the King,
and I will bless Thy name forever and ever.
* 2 Every day will I bless Thee,
and I will praise Thy name forever and ever.
* 3 Great is the LORD, and greatly to be praised,
and His greatness is unsearchable.

* 4 One generation shall commend Thy works to another,
and they shall declare Thy mighty acts.
* 5 They shall speak of the splendour of the glory of Thy majesty,
and meditate on Thy wondrous works.
* 6 And they shall speak of the power of Thy terrible deeds,
and recount Thy greatness.
* 7 They shall pour forth the memory of Thy
abundant goodness,
and ring out their joy at Thy justice.

* 8 The LORD is gracious and compassionate,
slow to anger and of great mercy.
* 9 The LORD is good to all,
and His compassion is upon all His works.

* 10 Let all Thy works thank Thee, O LORD,
and let Thy saints bless Thee.
* 11 Let them speak of the glory of Thy kingdom,
and tell of Thy might:
* 12 To make known to the sons of men Thy mighty deeds,
and the glory of the splendour of Thy kingdom.
* 13 Thy kingdom is a kingdom for all ages,
and Thy dominion is throughout all generations.

* The LORD is faithful in all His words,
and merciful in all His works.
* 14 The LORD holdeth up all that fall,
and raiseth up all that are bowed down.

* 15 The eyes of all wait upon Thee,
and Thou givest them their food in due season.
* 16 Thou openest Thy hand
and satisfiest the good pleasure of every living thing.

* 17 The LORD is just in all His ways,
and merciful in all His works.
* 18 The LORD is near to all that call upon Him,
to all that call upon Him in truth.

* 19 He will do the will of those that fear Him,
and He will hear their cry for help and save them.
* 20 The LORD keepeth all that love Him,
but all the wicked He will destroy.

* 21 My mouth shall speak the praise of the LORD, †
and let all flesh bless His holy name
forever and ever.

Psalm 146 (145)

Lau• a, anima

"There is no salvation in any other" (Acts 4:12)

* 1 Alleluia.
Praise the LORD, O my soul.
* 2 I will praise the LORD while I live;
I will sing psalms to my God while I have my being.

* 3 Put not your trust in princes,
in a son of man, in whom there is no salvation.
* 4 His spirit shall depart, he shall return to his earth;
on that very day, his thoughts perish.

* 5 Blessed he whose help is the God of Jacob,
whose expectation is in the LORD his God,
* 6 Who made heaven and earth,
the sea and all that is in them.

* Who keepeth truth forever;
7 Who executeth judgment for the oppressed;
* Who giveth bread to the hungry;
the LORD looseth the prisoners.

* 8 The LORD openeth the eyes of the blind;
the LORD raiseth up those that are bowed down;
* the LORD loveth the just;
9 the LORD keepeth the sojourners.
* The fatherless and the widow He will lift up,
but the way of the wicked He will make crooked.

* 10 The LORD will reign forever, †
thy God, O Zion, from generation to generation.
Alleluia.

Psalm 147 (146: 1-11; 147)

Lau• ate Dominum

"He will...gather His elect from the four winds" (Mark 13:27)

* 1 Alleluia! †
For it is good to sing psalms to our God;
for pleasant is fitting praise.

* 2 The LORD buildeth up Jerusalem;
He will gather the dispersed of Israel:
* 3 He Who healeth the brokenhearted,
and bindeth up their wounds;
* 4 Who counteth out the number of the stars,
Who calleth them all by their names.

* 5 Great is our LORD, and abundant in power;
of His understanding there is no number.
* 6 The LORD lifteth up the meek;
He humbleth the wicked to the ground.

* 7 O sing to the LORD in thanksgiving;
sing psalms to our God upon the harp.

* 8 Who covereth the heavens with clouds;
Who prepareth rain for the earth;
* Who maketh grass to grow upon the mountains,
and herbs for the service of man;
* 9 Who giveth to the beasts their food,
to the young ravens when they call.

* 10 He delighteth not in the strength of the horse,
nor is He well pleased with the legs of a man.
* 11 The LORD is well pleased with those that fear Him,
with those that hope in His mercy.

* 12 Laud the LORD, O Jerusalem;
praise thy God, O Zion.

* 13 For He hath strengthened the bars of thy gates;
He hath blessed thy children within thee.
* 14 Who maketh peace thy border;
He satisfieth thee with the fat of wheat.
* 15 Who sendeth forth His utterance to the earth:
His word runneth swiftly.

* 16 Who giveth snow like wool;
frost He scattereth like ashes.
* 17 He casteth forth His ice like morsels;
before the face of His cold who can stand?
* 18 He sendeth forth His word and melteth them;
He maketh His wind blow, and the waters flow.

* 19 He declareth His word to Jacob,
His statutes and judgments to Israel.
* 20 He hath not done so to all the Gentiles;
they have not known His judgments. Alleluia.

Psalm 148

Laudate Dominum de caelis

"The Love that moves the sun and the other stars"

(Dante, *Divine Comedy*, conclusion)

* 1 Alleluia. †
Praise the LORD from the heavens;
praise Him in the heights;
* 2 Praise Him, all ye His angels;
praise Him, all ye His hosts.
* 3 Praise Him sun and moon;
praise Him all ye stars of light.
* 4 Praise Him ye heavens of heavens,
and ye waters that are above the heavens:

* 5 Let them praise the name of the LORD,
for He commanded and they were created.

* 6 And He made them stand forever and ever;
He gave a statute, and it will not pass away.

* 7 Praise the LORD from the earth,
ye sea dragons and all deeps,
* 8 fire and hail, snow and smoke,
stormy wind, executing His word.
* 9 Mountains and all hills,
fruit trees and all cedars,
* 10 beasts and all cattle,
creeping things and wingèd birds.
* 11 Kings of the earth and all peoples,
princes and all judges of the earth,
* 12 men, and also maidens,
the old together with the young:

* 13 Let them praise the name of the LORD, †
for His name alone is exalted.
His majesty is above earth and heaven.

* 14 And He hath exalted the horn of His people,
praise for all His saints,
* for the children of Israel,
a people near to Him. Alleluia.

Psalm 149

Cantate Domino

"The saints shall judge the world"
(1 Corinthians 6:2; cf. Apocalypse 20:4a)

* 1 Alleluia. †
Sing to the LORD a new song;
His praise is in the church of the saints.
* 2 Let Israel rejoice in Him that made him;
let the children of Zion exult in their king.
* 3 Let them praise His name with dancing;
with timbrel and harp, let them sing psalms to Him.

* 4 For the LORD is well pleased with His people;
He will adorn the meek with salvation.
* 5 Let the saints exult in glory;
let them ring out their joy upon their couches.
* 6 Let the high praises of God be in their throat,
and a two-edged sword in their hand.

* 7 To execute vengeance upon the nations,
chastisements upon the peoples;
* 8 to bind their kings with chains,
and their nobles with fetters of iron;
* 9 to execute on them the judgment written:
This is the splendour of all His saints. Alleluia.

Psalm 150

Lau• ate Dominum in sanctis

A summons to universal praise

* 1 Alleluia. †
Praise God in His sanctuary;
praise Him in the firmament of His strength.
* 2 Praise Him in His mighty acts;
praise Him according to the abundance of His greatness.

* 3 Praise Him with the sound of the trumpet;
praise Him with psaltery and harp.
* 4 Praise Him with timbrel and dance;
praise Him with strings and pipe.
* 5 Praise Him with sweet-sounding cymbals;
praise Him with loud-clashing cymbals:

* Let all breath
praise the LORD. Alleluia.

APPENDIX

Revise• Rheims Gospel Canticles

Te Deum (Revise• from A. Fortescue)

Weekly Psalm Scheme

Three Images

BENEDICTUS

Canticle of Zachary (Luke 1:68-79)

Greeting the long-expected dawn of redemption

(cf. Zechariah 3:8 and 6:12, Greek)

* 68 Blesséd be the Lord, the God of Israel,
for He hath visited and wrought redemption for His people;
* 69 and He hath raised up a horn of salvation for us
in the house of His servant David.

* 70 As He spoke by the mouth of His holy prophets from of old, †
71 salvation from our enemies
and from the hand of all that hate us,
* 72 to perform mercy with our fathers,
and to remember His holy covenant,

* 73 the oath He swore to Abraham our father †
that He would grant us, that we,
74 being delivered from the hand of our enemies,
* 75 might serve Him without fear,
in holiness and justice before Him all our days.

* 76 And thou, child, shalt be called †
the prophet of the Most High,
for thou shalt go before the face of the Lord
to prepare His ways,
* 77 to give knowledge of salvation to His people
by the forgiveness of their sins,

* 78 through the tender mercy of our God,
whereby the Orient from on high shall visit us,
* 79 to enlighten those that sit in darkness
and the shadow of death,
to direct our feet into the way of peace.

MAGNIFICAT

Canticle of Mary (Luke 1:46-55; cf. 1 Samuel 2:1-10)

Marveling at the providential vicissitudes of salvation history

* 46 My soul doth magnify the Lord, †
47 and my spirit hath rejoiced in God my Saviour,
48 because He hath regarded the humility of His handmaid.

* For behold from henceforth all generations shall call me blesséd, †
49 because He Who is powerful hath done great things for me, and holy is His name;
* 50 and His mercy is from generation to generation
to those that fear Him:

* 51 He hath done mighty deeds with His arm;
He hath scattered the proud in the conceit of their heart.
* 52 He hath pulled down potentates from thrones,
and exalted the humble.
* 53 He hath filled the hungry with good things,
and the rich He hath sent empty away.

* 54 He hath helped His servant Israel,
being mindful of His mercy,
* 55 even as He spoke to our fathers,
to Abraham and to his seed forever.

NUNC DIMITTIS

Canticle of Simeon (Luke 2:29-32)

"His father and mother wondered at what was said of him"
(Luke 2:33)

* 29 Now dost Thou dismiss Thy servant, O Master,
according to Thy word, in peace;

* 30 because my eyes have seen Thy salvation,
31 which Thou hast prepared before the face of all peoples:

* 32 A light for revelation to the Gentiles,
and the glory of Thy people Israel.

TE DEUM

* 1 Thee, O God, do we praise;
we confess Thee to be the Lord.
* 2 All the earth doth worship Thee,
the Father everlasting.

* 3 To Thee all the angels,
to Thee the heavens, and the universal powers,
* 4 to Thee the cherubim and seraphim
with unceasing voice do cry:

* 5 Holy, holy, holy,
Lord God of hosts.
* 6 Heaven and earth are full
of the majesty of Thy glory.

* 7 Thee the glorious choir of the apostles, †
8 Thee the praiseworthy band of the prophets,
9 Thee the white-robed army of martyrs do praise.
* 10 Thee the holy Church
throughout all the world doth confess:
* 11 The Father of boundless majesty, †
12 Thy adorable, true, and only Son,
13 and also the Holy Ghost the Paraclete.

* 14 Thou art the king of glory, O Christ.
15 Thou art the everlasting Son of the Father.
* 16 Thou, having taken upon Thee to liberate man,
didst not disdain the Virgin's womb.
* 17 Having overcome the sting of death,
Thou didst open the kingdom of heaven to believers.
* 18 Thou sittest at the right hand of God
in the glory of the Father.
* 19 We believe Thee to be
the judge that is to come.

* [20] We beseech Thee, therefore, assist Thy servants,
whom Thou hast redeemed with Thy precious blood.
* [21] Make them to be numbered with Thy saints
in glory everlasting.

* [22] O Lord, save Thy people,
and bless Thy inheritance.
* [23] And govern them,
and exalt them forever.

* [24] Day by day we bless Thee, †
[25] and we praise Thy name forever—
indeed, world without end.

* [26] Vouchsafe, O Lord, this day
to keep us without sin.
* [27] O Lord, have mercy upon us,
have mercy upon us.

* [28] O Lord, let Thy mercy be upon us,
even as we have hoped in Thee.
* [29] In Thee, O Lord, have I hoped:
let me not be confounded forever.

MONASTIC SCHEME B FOR THE WEEKLY PSALTER

Day	Invitatory	Matins		Lauds	Terce	Sext	None	Vespers	Compline
Sun.	81	110 18 2	45 9-10 72	93 3 30 147	119: 1-32	118	136	113 114 115 116	4 91 134
Mon.	29	1 104 (70) 71	94 105 112	100 63 101 135	119: 33-56	25	120 121 122	33 61 28 48	34
Tue.	67	6 107 7	74 73 77 (108)	98 90 65 117	119: 57-80	42- 43	123 124 125	75 140 26 145	139
Wed.	46	78 132	19 58 49 82	97 36 57 149	119: 81-104	44	126 127 128	103 86 85 87	32 62 133
Thu.	24	39 37 41	50 68 83	47 76 5 148	119: 105-128	55	129 130 131	111 23 84 40	102
Fri.	8	88 69 38	60 106 79	96 143 64 146	119: 129-152	22	11 12 13 (14)	144 141 142 27	31
Sat.	95	59 109 56	137 89 80	99 51 92 150	119: 153-176	35	52 53 54	66 20 21 138	15 17 16

Note: Psalms 14, 70 and 108 have been inserted in parenthesis to complete the 150 Psalms.

Father Gregory Martin (1540-1582)

Translator of the Douay-Rheims Bible

William Cardinal Allen (1532-1594)

Sponsor of the Douay-Rheims Bible

Bishop Richard Challoner (1691-1781)

Reviser of the Douay-Rheims Bible, who first issued its Old and New Testaments in a single volume

Made in the USA
Las Vegas, NV
01 December 2023